Also by Harry Eyres

Plato's "The Republic": A Beginner's Guide

Hotel Eliseo

Cabernet Sauvignon

*Wine Dynasties of Europe: Personal Portraits of Ten
Leading Houses*

Horace and Me

Horace and Me

Life Lessons from an Ancient Poet

Harry Eyres

Farrar, Straus and Giroux

New York

Farrar, Straus and Giroux
18 West 18th Street, New York 10011

The passage on pages 51–52 is from Lucius Junius Moderatus
Columella, *Of Husbandry in Twelve Books: And His Book Concerning
Trees*, Book III, Chapter III; translated anonymously; printed for
A. Millar, London, 1745.

Grateful acknowledgment is made for permission to reprint the poem
"Whale Burial" by Harry Eyres, from *Hotel Eliseo* (Hearing Eye, 2001).

Library of Congress Cataloging-in-Publication Data
Eyres, Harry, 1958–
   Horace and me : life lessons from an ancient poet / Harry Eyres. —
First edition.
      pages   cm
   ISBN 978-0-374-17274-9 (alk. paper)
   1. Horace—Criticism and interpretation.   2. Horace—Influence.
3. Poetry—Influence.   I. Title.

PA6411.E97 2013
874'.01—dc23
                                                    2012048085

Designed by Jonathan D. Lippincott

www.fsgbooks.com
www.twitter.com/fsgbooks • www.facebook.com/fsgbooks

1   3   5   7   9   10   8   6   4   2

*Frontispiece: The statue of Horace by Achille D'Orsi
in the Piazza Orazio, Venosa*

To my father, who lived and tasted
the day to the very end

THE SACRIFICE (ODES 3.13)

O holy spring, Bandusia, clear one
Brighter than any man-made crystal
Let me sprinkle sweet wine over your waters,
And a bouquet of wildflowers.

Tomorrow I'll sacrifice a kid to you
A youngling, horns budding, all ready
For love and war, a bundle
Of life and lust, but doomed:

His warm red blood will stain your
Pristine, icy water, which demands
Nothing less than an entire life
Of one cut off from the flock.

In recompense you give all this:
Your lovely saving coolness which
No heat or war can touch,
Which the exhausted and the lost can drink.

And I will sing you into immortality
Speaking of the holm-oak growing
From your hollow rocks, the endless
Babble where your waters leap.

Contents

A Note on the Translations   xi

1. More Durable than Bronze   3
2. Coming Back to Horace   11
3. The Soul of Wine   31
4. Among the Centurions' Sons   53
5. The Scholars   69
6. "I Set Out Alone"   79
7. The Freedom of the Poet   93
8. Love, Friendship, Therapy   103
9. Town Mouse and Country Mouse   133
10. Religion, or How to Believe   165
11. Carpe Diem   183
12. Excess, or Enough   197
13. In the South   209
14. Alas, the Years   225

Acknowledgments   237

A Note on the Translations

All the translations from Horace, and all but one of the Catullus translations, are by me. The verse translations from Horace and Catullus are, strictly speaking, versions, rather than literal translations. My aim has been, in Ezra Pound's terms, to make the poems new. The first rule is that the versions have to live, to hold the reader, as contemporary poems, not museum pieces. The second rule is that they should keep as much of Horace's sense, imagery, tone, and music as possible, or as much as the first rule allows. I haven't tried to reproduce Horace's wonderful intricate original meters with any exactitude because that does not seem to be compatible with the first rule. One obvious sticking point is mythology—in particular the glancing references to mythological stories and figures that Horace assumed his audience would know. There is no simple solution to that, but I have cut out certain references that seemed too obscure to make any sense without tedious elaboration. I have also, at times, replaced classical references with modern ones; in Odes 3.21, for instance, I have substituted Supermac (Harold Macmillan) for Consul Manlius, so that Horace's wine jar, vintaged in the year of his birth, becomes my own contemporary and twin. In Odes 3.29, I have brought in references to the war in Iraq instead of uprisings on the borders of the Roman Empire. Again there is Ezra Pound's precedent for this: the reference in "Homage to Sextus Propertius," his collage of Propertius fragments, to "a frigidaire patent." In all this I have been guided not by any consistent doctrine or theory but by rules of thumb based on an instinct for what makes a piece of writing feel alive rather than dead. I hope I have Horace's authority for that.

Horace and Me

More Durable than Bronze

Once again I'm taking this small object through airport security and I'm wondering whether any of the machines will pick it up. Probably not. Though the contents are described as "more durable than bronze" and in terms of half-life rival any radioactive isotope, they don't set off any contemporary alarms. Our systems are geared toward mobile phones and computers, shoe bombs and booby-trapped undergarments. My object is made of metaphorical metal and its power and capacity cannot be measured in volts or gigabytes.

This thing is red in color and measures a little over six inches by four inches by one inch. It is in fact a book—an old Loeb Library edition that contains a hundred and twenty poems written two thousand years ago by the Roman poet Horace. One hundred and three of those poems are arranged in four books of odes (Horace actually used the word *carmina*, meaning songs), the work of which the poet was proudest, and which he thought would guarantee his immortality.

Placing this small battered book on my airport café table, looking out over tarmac-covered runways, some woods beyond them, a gray English morning sky, makes me feel more moored and anchored in a place whose very essence is hypermobility. Moored to what? To myself, to some depth of feeling in myself.

Reading this particular poem, the thirtieth and last of Book

Three, in which Horace prophesies that his odes will outlast the pyramids, is affecting me so much that I am afraid I may start weeping, or generally betray the kind of emotion you are not supposed to show in airport cafés.

Horace is making a pretty outrageous claim. He is saying that these poems are time-proof—proof against floods and hurricanes, or just the drip-drip of steady rain and the passing of the uncounted days, weeks, months, "the unnumbered series of years and the flight of time." The extraordinary thing is that he was right; he wrote his poems into the future, for the future as much as for the present, and they remain always contemporary. The scholars who try to nail Horace, and other ancient authors who still speak to us, down to the past have got something fundamentally wrong.

"Not all of me will die; part of me will escape the goddess of death." Maybe that's what's affecting me. Something to counter the fear of death that attends all airports, all flights into the unknown. I'm only flying to Turin (as it happens), but this is the place of departures and sometime soon they'll call my flight; my number will come. The mobile phone rings; it's my partner wishing me a safe flight, reminding me to drink enough water. She's right; I need water. But not water alone; I also need Horace, who said no poetry worth reading was written by drinkers of water. Just for a moment I weigh the sleek metal coolness of the phone against the warmer, frayed old book. In terms of apparent power, attractiveness, usefulness, surely the gleaming gizmo wins out (not that it's a new phone, or a smartphone—any self-respecting teenager would regard it as an antique). I wonder which will have the longer future.

I am reminded of a phrase from a newspaper article I recently added to my cuttings file in which the historian Timothy Garton Ash criticized the thoughtless stereotyping of Poles as anti-Semitic. He went on to characterize "the language of today's party politics" as consisting of "prefabricated phrases and glib half-truths." Such phrases and half-truths cannot be expected to last long. They are not made of the right durable stuff, for a start. Their foundations are not deep. They don't bear any profound relation to reality, or true emotion. When a big storm or disaster strikes, they fall apart, smashed to useless tinder.

Wandering into the airport bookshop, I notice the volume by the British Liberal Democrat minister Vince Cable entitled *The Storm*. The cover shows Cable looking suitably gloomy and also prophetic, against a backdrop of ominous clouds. His book is about the economic storm that hit the western economies apparently without much warning in 2008. For a few days or weeks in September and October of that year, following the collapse of the American bank Lehman Brothers, it looked as if the entire system of credit that lubricated the globalized capitalist system was seizing up.

I happened to be having lunch with a very important personage on one of those October days, when the U.K.'s Royal Bank of Scotland, the world's largest bank at that time, very nearly went bust. That would have meant money not coming out of ATM machines, people unable to pay for food, riots on the streets. My friend, a director of the bank, gamely went ahead with the lunch, during which we talked about the English Hispanist Gerald Brenan and our shared love of Spanish culture, but I could see he had turned pale and that he was hardly touching his food. If someone like him was worried, I reflected, we really must be in trouble.

Since then the crisis has rolled on, deepening rather than resolving itself. As my friend predicted, what began as a financial crisis would become an economic one. Cable was right; the storm clouds really did seem to be gathering. After decades in which the lucky people of the earth felt things were only getting better, could only get better, the kind of conditions that created the Great Depression of the 1930s, with the terrible consequences we all know, suddenly didn't seem so distant. And they were being exacerbated by politicians who appeared to have learned nothing from history, especially not the lessons of John Maynard Keynes. And as if all that was not bad enough, this financial and economic crisis was merely being added to an ongoing, and potentially far more grave, environmental crisis, in which the capacity of the earth, the oceans, the atmosphere to absorb industrial pollution, to sustain the conditions for tolerable life, was being put under serious threat. Here was a profound crisis not just of economy but of values, born of surfeit rather than penury: born of the excess of credit and consumption.

Strangely enough, I don't think any of this would have greatly surprised Horace. He too perceived a crisis of values in the midst of what appeared to be peace and plenty.

At last the civil wars, a period of almost unimaginable chaos and bloodshed, are over. The major foreign enemies have been defeated. There are no longer any limits, either of space or time. The word comes from on high that history has ended (Francis Fukuyama's version), or "dominion without end is my gift to you" (Jupiter's words to Aeneas in Book 1 of Virgil's *Aeneid*). The empire has dawned; a sun has risen that will not set.

And yet, just at this moment of supreme temporal triumph come obscure rumors of defeat. Legions are stranded abroad. Daring attacks threaten the impregnable capital city. Immense material wealth proves strangely counterproductive; it even seems to consume itself. City dwellers are deafened by noise, suffocated by smog. Even the fish in the ocean feel their environment contracting, hemmed in by concrete fish pens that extend human dominion into the ownerless deep.

Horace's time and ours are linked by a curious sense of hollowness at the heart of unparalleled prosperity. The old gods are abandoning the city, just when their guidance might be needed most. Surrounded by skyscrapers, palaces, fed full with delicacies and entertainments, people feel adrift, their moorings gone. Though a relatively peaceful political order has been established, there is a deep crisis of values that threatens to undermine that order.

For a long time now no one sophisticated has taken the old gods, the old religion, or the archaic virtues of frugality and simplicity particularly seriously. God has been turned into money, and money has amazing powers; no gates or guardians can stop it; it can bribe and destroy states. But to the keenest sensibility of the age, materialism itself, which seemed so solid, is revealed as a false god. Growing affluence appears to breed only an insatiable hunger for more, a desolate sense of something always lacking.

Horace asked himself, just as we are asking ourselves, these questions: What exactly is this new dominion, empire, or global new order? Can it offer unlimited peace and prosperity, stretching forward into infinite horizons of time, or does it consist of little more than a soulless efficiency, an instrumentalism that makes everything a means to an end, with the end itself lost along the way? In which case, might not the greatest loss and poverty be of time itself, the lived and living moment, the day, which is the gods' gift to us, but which is always being sacrificed to a more glorious tomorrow?

Horace's response to living in his time of global power threatened by its inner vacuum of values, not so unlike our time of global capitalism, in which no value other than the monetary is recognized, was to be contrary. The life work he set himself, writing a body of Latin lyric poetry in Greek meters, could be seen as supremely useless. Though he managed to persuade himself that Augustus's new order was benign, he railed against plutocracy and declared himself on the side of those with little, while recognizing that he was compromised, a friend to rich men as well as to the poor.

He insisted on the benefits to be gained from recognizing inescapable limits: the limit to human life; the sanity of being satisfied with "what is enough," rather than the restless reaching after more; the happiness of dwelling in "one dear perpetual place," rather than being constantly on the move but never escaping what you cannot leave behind, yourself.

Horace's warning to jet-setters comes at the end of his verse letter to Bullatius: "You can change the color of the sky, not the color of your mind / By jetting over oceans; a sort of busy idleness wears us out; / We think the best way to live is to buy a yacht or an SUV; / Everything you need is here, in Pitsville, if your mind is sane."

At last my flight is called. I put the small battered book away in its usual pocket in my rucksack and proceed toward the gate. I wonder whether I am inflating the book's value, putting more onto it than it can bear. But then the book and its author never claimed they could solve any great practical challenge, like throwing a water supply across a valley, or lifting a hundred tons of metal five miles into the air.

What I have in my rucksack, as I move along the walkway toward the marvel of modern technology that will transport me (I hope) over seas and mountains, is just some debris from a long-gone civilization. But it is, as I hope this book will show, a magical sort of debris, the equal and opposite of the nuclear waste that will remain toxic for thousands of years.

Horace is the canniest of classics, able to survive in fragmentary form. He invented some of the pithiest phrases ever coined. Horace's phrases, lines, and poems have lasted, I reckon, because they're the opposite of prefabricated or glib. His words are put together with a carpentry or stonemasonry so cunning and precise that nothing can prize them apart. Syllables, sounds, rhythms are locked together with a force that even earthquakes could not budge.

And they are not just decorative. Horace once said that poetry should be both sweet and useful. Or even true.

The Horatian Spanish poet Antonio Machado defined poetry as "a few true words," a definition that sounds minimal, even despairing, until you reflect on what a few true words can do. They might help us find our bearings, keep us on track, in a world, a universe, that seems to get vaster and more mystifying but not more navigable as knowledge without wisdom proliferates. At least they have helped me find my bearings and keep myself on track. Just now, I'm hoping they'll see me through to Turin, and beyond.

Two

Coming Back to Horace

This is a story of how I came back to Horace—and came back to myself at the same time. It is a story of how the very thing that almost deadened me—that is, classical education and literature epitomized by Horace—turned out to be a secret savior, a way of orienting myself back to myself, to some kind of sanity. What if the thing that helped save me and reorient me might help save others, even an entire civilization?

Not only I was lost. Horace was lost too—through no fault of his own. He had become lost partly by becoming too successful. For centuries Horace had been the classic of classics—the man, the paragon of sanity, the guru of the golden mean you turned to when you needed advice on how to write or how to live. Profoundly admired by writers as different as Petrarch and Voltaire, Pope and Johnson, Goethe and Nietzsche, Horace had ended up being caricatured as a sort of smiling English squire. And then when a certain idea of the world and of civilization came crashing down in 1914, Horace was fingered as one of the culprits.

Few poets have ever stuck the knife in deeper to a fellow poet than Wilfred Owen, writing from the trenches of the First World War in the fierce poem entitled "Dulce et decorum est," which ends, quoting Horace's unforgivable line ("It is sweet and fitting to die for one's country"), like this:

If you could hear, at every jolt, the blood
Come gargling from the froth-corrupted lungs,
Obscene as cancer, bitter as the cud
Of vile incurable sores on innocent tongues,—
My friend, you would not tell with such high zest
To children ardent for some desperate glory,
The Old Lie—dulce et decorum est
Pro patria mori.

At a stroke Horace became the smug representative of imperialism, the éminence grise who sent millions of young men to ghastly deaths.

For postwar iconoclasts such as Ezra Pound and the members of the Bloomsbury Group, Horace was the problem, not the solution. Much more attractive than Horace's measured, ambivalent support of Augustus's Pax Romana were romantic young rebels such as Catullus, who said he did not care whether Caesar was pale or swarthy, or Propertius, who daringly looked forward to much later poets such as John Donne by making his mistress, not his emperor, the center of everything—or Ovid, who ended up being exiled by the emperor for writing risqué verses that did not fit with Augustus's hypocritical "back to basics" moral agenda.

Catullus, Propertius, and Ovid were more attractive to me too as a schoolboy. Horace seemed the most distant and ungraspable of all the Roman poets. I didn't entirely trust him—too suave, too close to power.

But the establishment Horace was a falsification, a travesty. The real Horace would turn out to be an infinitely more complex, poised, critical figure; how else would he have appealed so strongly to so many of the West's most enlightened and critical spirits, who usually identified him with the struggle for intellectual freedom against all forms of dogmatism?

As I trace my own story in these pages, from confusion and disorientation to a kind of orientation (which doesn't mean self-satisfaction but having a sense of where you are tending), I also hope to put the picture straighter regarding Horace, one of the clearest poetic intelligences who ever lived, and one of the West's lost prophets.

If I, in common with many writers over the past two millennia, have come to regard Horace as a friend, he is obviously an unlikely one: not so much an imaginary friend as an impossible one. How could anyone who lived more than two thousand years ago, in the time of togas, have more than the remotest connection to someone born into the late-twentieth- and early-twenty-first-century world of jets and phones, of Twitter and Facebook? Our starts in life were certainly very different. Horace was born in southern Italy, in the town of Venusia, on the borders of two provinces, which we now call Puglia and Basilicata, and which the Romans called Apulia and Lucania. And he was born if not on the wrong side of the tracks, then in decidedly modest circumstances. Horace's father, as he tells us again and again, almost relentlessly, as if because he cannot forget it we should not either, was a freed slave.

Now the word "slave," for us, has all sorts of connotations that are misleading in terms of Roman society in the first century B.C. We are bound to think of men and women shackled and transported like animals, forced to work in inhuman conditions, treated with casual brutality.

Roman slavery was not like that at all—or not necessarily like that. Of course it could be brutal; the conditions in the gold and silver mines of Hispania were presumably no better than those in the terrible mines of Potosí. But then all sorts of professions we consider perfectly respectable—teaching, hairdressing, tailoring—were practiced in Roman society by slaves. Many inhabitants of Italian towns conquered by Rome in the Social War of 91–88 B.C.—possibly including Horace's father—were taken into slavery. And Roman slavery had one feature uncommon in other slave-owning societies: it was not necessarily for life; slaves could buy their freedom. Freed slaves could and did prosper, though they could not hold political office.

We don't know exactly why Horace's father became a slave, but we do know that he bought his freedom. And we know, or can deduce, that he did well for himself as a small businessman or auctioneer (Suetonius in his *Life of Horace* says he was a seller of salt fish, but that may be apocryphal): well enough to send his brilliant son—who, it appears, was his only child, and whom he apparently brought up on his own—to be educated under one of the most fashionable teachers in Rome.

Now Horace's story and mine are beginning to converge, as far as that is possible two millennia apart.

Unlike Horace, I was brought up in a family that rather looked down on social aspiration. Socially, it seemed we had made it; we could examine our lineage in a volume called *Burke's Landed Gentry*; we lived in what a guide to our small village in the English Home Counties called one of its "gentleman's residences." My father's ancestors, for a couple of centuries or so, had been officers in the navy, or ambassadors, or fellows of Oxbridge colleges turned country vicars. The one whose portrait still hangs in my parents' drawing room, George Bolton Eyres, had reached the rank of major-general in the East India Company army. Who knows what kind of wheeler-dealering, backed by military force, he had employed to pay for the handsome house near Bath, seen in the background of the portrait of his wife?

In a sort of Jane Austen world we occupied a rung of society high enough not to be too preoccupied by social ambitions. It was probably the rung the Old Etonian socialist writer George Orwell identified with comic precision as lower-upper-middle class.

In our very different social milieus, growing up at different times in world history, we had certain things in common. One was at least one parent (my mother, Horace's father) preoccupied almost to obsession with education, and literary education in particular.

Another was the shadow of war. Horace actually lived through a civil war and fought in one of the ancient world's bloodiest battles, the battle of Philippi in 42 B.C. And he fought not on the side of the eventual winners, but on the side of the losers, the defenders of the Roman Republic, Brutus and Cassius. Horace, like many other privileged young Romans studying in Athens, had been caught up in the idealistic fervor that followed the murder, or tyrannicide, of Julius Caesar. To get close to a modern equivalent, you would have to go back to the Spanish Civil War and those who went out to fight for the Republic.

I was lucky, again, in comparison to him; privileged in social class and having the fortune to avoid the world wars of the twentieth century. Even my father, joining the British army in 1944, missed the fighting, though not the experience of seeing what area bombing had done to the city of Hamburg. That experience would have a profound influence on his life.

Horace, having lived his early life in the shadow, and at times in the thick, of violent civil war, spent his mature years in the relative peace and affluence of the reign of the first Roman emperor, Augustus (who did not call himself emperor, precisely, but *princeps*, first among the citizens). It was not a peace and affluence without shadows and alarms; Horace's own poetry reveals how much anxiety attended even the high noon of Roman power. The Odes, which celebrate the plenitude of living in the day, are shadowed by the offstage quaking of vassal kings.

To him it seemed infinitely preferable to the appalling internecine bloodletting of the previous decades. For that reason, he came to be a supporter of the Augustan regime—an unforgivable crime in the eyes of romantics. Once upon a time I disliked him for it too.

But Horace's position was not one of uncritical support. In fact the longer and deeper I have looked into the infinitely deep waters of his poetry, the more I have come to appreciate the complex tension of the position Horace came to adopt.

Horace was first and foremost a poet. That sounds almost too obvious to mention. But what lies behind it, what it really means, is not obvious at all. Simply to carve out a space for lyric poetry in a pragmatic, increasingly instrumental and money-driven society was an immense, even heroic achievement. The scale and the heroism of the achievement can be measured by the fact that as a Roman lyric poet, strictly speaking, that is, one who used the Greek lyric meters, Horace had only one significant predecessor—Catullus in just a handful of lyrics—and a few imitators, but no real successors. No wonder he could look back on his achievement in the last poem of Odes 1–3, arguably the most influential collection of lyrics ever published, and say he had built a monument destined to last longer than all the pompous and pretentious architectural grandiosities of the age. A perilously boastful claim; but Horace was right.

To comprehend what he meant and why he said it, you need to reflect on why lyric poetry matters. This is a major theme and concern of this book, of mine and of Horace's; and Horace, who for two thousand years has stood as the epitome of lyric poetry in the West, is one of its most eloquent advocates.

Defending lyric poetry and its space in a sophisticated society has always needed a combination of fervor and irony. Pope had it right when he wrote of Horace that "he judg'd with Coolness, tho' he sung with fire." Already in Horace's time the poet with his lyre is in some ways an anachronistic figure. If poets in the West from the Renaissance onward have looked back to Horace, then Horace was always looking back to Greece, to the lyric poets of the islands of Lesbos and Paros in the seventh century B.C., to Sappho and Alcaeus and Archilochus—and to Pindar, writing victory odes at the height of Athens's glory.

The idea that such a figure as the lyric poet could be important, even essential, in a big, brash world of legions and plutocrats, aqueducts and underfloor heating, is hard to sell. What use or power does a little poem have, set against world-changing developments in military hardware, or civil engineering, or medicine? No poem ever saved a single life. Or so it might seem, if you are being literal. Which of course is the last thing poems are.

A substantial part of my life has been devoted to the quixotic task of defending lyric poetry and its essential humanizing space. I write poetry, sporadically (I wish the muses visited me more regularly, but there we are). I have been a teacher of poetry and I was proud to serve for four years as the poetry editor of a national newspaper—a tabloid newspaper, as it happened, whose readers revealed an unexpected appetite for verse. In my present incarnation I try to set at least one of the pink pages of the *Financial Times* rustling with a breeze whose stirrings start on Parnassus, not in the Paris bourse or the London Stock Exchange or Wall Street.

Poetry in our time has been reduced to the status of a harmless hobby, like stamp collecting or kite flying. It is a fun activity for children, or a form of escapism. I take a different view. I stand with Ezra Pound, who said, "It is essential that great poetry be written," who saw poets and artists as the "antennae of the race." In my loftier moments I even stand with Wallace Stevens, who wrote in *Opus Posthumous* that "after one has abandoned a belief in god, poetry is that essence which takes its place as life's redemption."

Lyric poetry—the most personal, subjective kind of poetry, whose subject matter is the poet's life, loves, hatreds, losses—has a special place even within what we might think of (wrongly) as the already rarefied world of poetry. It is, if you like, the purest kind of poetry, poetry tout court. Lyric poems are short, or shortish, which is already a kind of statement in a world given to grandiosity, where in general big is beautiful.

Horace consistently refused to write epic poetry, the big, grand kind of poetry that his big, grand age seemed to call for, and which his close friend Virgil, not without huge misgivings, eventually supplied. Virgil spent the last ten years of his life

composing the *Aeneid*, the epic about the foundation of Rome
by the Trojan hero Aeneas. But the enterprise did not end happily. Virgil, torn by self-doubt, never finished, or never finished
polishing the epic and asked that it be destroyed at his death.

Horace, in covert terms, warned his friend about the perils
of the task he had embarked on. He was aware of its dangers—
the danger above all, perhaps, of a kind of self-defeating grandeur, of excessive ambition; in one of the pithiest and funniest
and most memorable of all his pithy sayings, he mocked the kind
of grandiose project in which "the mountains go into labor, and a
silly little mouse is born."

Sticking to lyric carried its own dangers, of course. One was
that Roman lyric poetry would never be truly popular, would
never appeal to a wide audience—the kind of audience Virgil
had reached, surprisingly perhaps, in his first, immensely popular collection of pastoral poems, the Eclogues. There are indica-
tions that Horace was deeply hurt when the collection of which
he was proudest, the first three books of lyrical odes, the crowning glory of his life's work and one of the crowning glories of
Western civilization, was not a popular triumph and achieved at
most a succès d'estime.

Another danger was that lyric would be seen as hedonistic,
effete, not really useful. Horace plays with that idea throughout
his odes, often in the form of an explicit or implicit dialogue with
his friend and patron, the dedicatee of the first book of odes,
Augustus's right-hand man and the second-most important man
of the empire, Maecenas. Time and again, almost provocatively,
Horace tells Maecenas that he will not be writing a bloody account of some Roman battle or campaign; he will leave that to
others. He will be writing about the charms of a slave girl (remember what we said earlier about slaves), or a good bottle of wine, or
a particular natural spring, never before celebrated by poets.

Behind this provocation and apparent flippancy, there is an
immensely serious message. Horace's point is that it is precisely

the apparently small things of life, the things you might take for granted, the view of that familiar hill, a sip of the wine that has restored you many times before, the way that girl has done up her hair, so simple and yet artful at the same time, that are the most important.

Normally in lyric poetry this message is subliminal or unconscious. The lyric poetry we are most familiar with is the product of young men and young women amplifying the pulse and strumming the strings of their own lives, immoderately lusting and loving and losing and not giving a cent (as Catullus put it) for the strictures of wise old asses.

Horace wrote his odes not in his twenties, the age at which Catullus and Donne wrote their love poetry, but in his later thirties and forties. They are the work of a middle-aged man, and all the richer and more complex and better for that (but I would say that, wouldn't I?).

People in their twenties are single-mindedly absorbed in being young, in feeling with that raw intensity that gradually and mercifully moderates into something more bearable. It would be rather odd and possibly unhealthy for a person in her twenties to spend much time thinking about being old. (Or at least when she did, she might come up with a purely romantic idea of what being old involves, as W. B. Yeats did when he began a poem with those beautiful, dreamy words, "When you are old and grey and full of sleep.")

But Horace's odes are as much concerned with old age as with youth. They are written from that privileged ridge of middle age from which you can see both slopes—the one you have climbed up so slowly and uncertainly from childhood, and the one you are destined to stumble down, all too quickly, toward the dark waters of the sluggish Styx. Horace wants to write about the whole of life, not just a small intense corner of it.

And what applies to age also applies to class. Horace was not just middle-aged when he wrote his odes, he was also in a very

particular position in terms of class, of his place in Roman society. Unlike Alcaeus and Catullus and John Donne, he was not
born into the upper classes. He knew what slavery was about,
because his father had been a slave.

Horace addresses his odes to rich and poor alike, to the lead-
ers of his society, to Maecenas and to other wealthy men, and to
slave boys and girls. The miraculously poised first book of odes
begins with a poem addressed to Maecenas and ends with one
addressed to a slave boy. It may be not exactly a question of
equality, but it is one of balance.

Horace wants to cover every angle, in a way that sometimes
seems positively Cubist, because he intends his poems to be not
pompous demonstrations of grandeur, like the pyramids (including the burial pyramid of his contemporary Caius Cestius), but
helpers of humanity. That is the secret of why he can say his
poems are "higher than the pyramids"; of course they are not
higher than the pyramids, they can all be contained in a little
book an inch thick, or nowadays a digital file less substantial than
the foreleg of a flea. But they are higher in an ethical sense.

What does it *take* to be or to become a lyric poet? Now there's
a question that cuts across the millennia. What did it take for Horace? It was not easy for him, it was a hard-won achievement, for
sure. It involved a certain kind of education, a classical education, a Greek education: that is something we will go into.

That is also something I share with Horace. I was one of the
last beneficiaries of an old-fashioned kind of classical education in
England that involved learning Latin and Greek, even learning to
compose verses in Latin hexameters and elegiac couplets and
Greek iambics. It seemed antiquated as I was going through it, and
it seems even more archaic now. Writing in my school magazine, I
questioned the stress on dead as opposed to living languages. Perhaps it was only after I had immersed myself in a living Latin
language, Spanish, that I was able to go back and make something

living out of the dead language I had been taught, often, I am afraid, in a deadly and deadening way. Somehow my classics instructors, teaching some of the most passionate, emotionally rich literature ever written, managed to turn much of it into sawdust.

For Horace it was different as, first, the languages he was studying were living, and, second, this was the education for gentlemen: there was no other. This was the education his father believed in and sacrificed all he had to give to his brilliant son. But I somehow doubt the auctioneer from Venusia had it in mind that his son would become a poet.

Being a poet, I reckon, has always involved some kind of renunciation, or even what Dante called "the great refusal." The Greek poet Cavafy transformed what in Dante's *Inferno* is a mark of shame into a badge of honor, the poet's badge:

CHE FECE . . . IL GRAN RIFIUTO

To a few people there comes a single day
When it is necessary to say the great Yes or the great
    No.
Immediately visible is the one who has the Yes
All ready in his center, and saying it

He steps into his honor and conviction.
The one who says no never regrets it—even if they
    asked
Again, he would say no again. All the same, that no,
The correct no, overwhelms him for the rest of his life.

tr. Harry Eyres

What is this "great refusal," or what was it for Horace, and what was it for me? Horace was clearly an exceptionally bright and able young man who could have succeeded in many callings. At the age of twenty-one he was a military tribune in the army of Brutus and Cassius, the equivalent of a colonel perhaps, an officer commanding a thousand men.

The decision to devote himself to poetry, and to lyric poetry in particular, may not have overwhelmed Horace but it marked him indelibly. He would have said it gave him freedom; the ease to get up late, wander around as his fancy took him, not be in an incessant stew about business or politics. It meant he followed in the great Greek philosophical tradition by valuing leisure above business.

Horace's success as a poet would bring him perilously close to those at the very apex of Roman power. What might seem Horace's greatest triumph, that the son of a freed slave should become a personal friend of the emperor, who writes about him in the most affectionate terms, addressing him as "purissimum penem," or "dear cock," could have been his downfall. It could have compromised his freedom, which was what Horace held most dear.

Augustus asked Horace to become his personal assistant, his letter writer (the emperor was an immensely assiduous correspondent), and Horace refused. This was "il gran rifiuto" with knobs on. I doubt Horace's father would have been happy about it. Surely this was the kind of offer you did not, could not, refuse. Horace even, for a long time, refused to write a poem addressed to Augustus. I think we can deduce from that that Horace did not really consider the emperor to be his friend (however the emperor regarded him), in the way that he considered Maecenas and Virgil and others to be his friends.

How Horace felt about this, about the risk of the loss of freedom, and how much freedom, the freedom of the poet, meant to him, he makes clear in an amazing passage in one of his verse letters or epistles. It is a reworking of a scene from the most stark and shattering of all Greek tragedies, the *Bacchae* by Euripides, in which the god Dionysus confronts the tyrant Pentheus.

In Horace's version it has become a confrontation between the good, wise man and his ruler. "What indignity will you make me suffer, King of Thebes?" asks the good, wise man. "I will take away your possessions." "You mean my cattle, my couches, my silver: take them." "I will place you in handcuffs and chains and hand you over to a torturer." "God himself will release me, as soon as I wish it."

This question of the poet's freedom has also preoccupied me. My "great refusal" was nothing as grand as choosing not to be the emperor's private secretary. It was more a series of refusals to do the kind of thing that my peers opted for. I tried, with no great conviction, to join the BBC and the Civil Service, and was not really surprised when they would not have me.

Once upon a time the BBC had employed the poet—and great admirer of Horace—Louis MacNeice as a producer, and asked him to sketch out his own schedule. When he left as many hours blank as filled he was asked what the blank spaces were for. "For thinking," he is said to have replied. At my final board in the Civil Service examination, I was faced with a semicircle of very serious-looking people wearing half-moon glasses. "What do you consider the gravest problem facing the U.K. at the moment, Mr. Eyres?" asked one of them, with solemn politeness. I blurted out what I felt but what I suspect was the wrong answer: "I think the fact that so many people do such dreadfully boring jobs."

I often felt I was much better at deciding what I did not want to do than what I wanted to do. Except that deep down I did know that I wanted to write; it was more that the way to achieve it was unclear to me.

I always seemed to need more time than most people, what Thoreau called a "broad margin" to my life. You could also say I wanted to relish time more. For me the freedom of the poet is essentially this: "time to stand and stare," as the Welsh poet W. H. Davies put it in "Leisure."

The freedom of the poet, which was what Horace held most dear, was both freedom of thought and freedom of action. No doubt freedom meant more to him than it might to another for the most deeply personal reasons.

For me the freedom of the poet is one aspect of a wider freedom: the freedom of the freelance writer. As long ago as the 1930s Louis MacNeice wrote, "Our freedom as free lances / Advances towards its end"; he meant this in the context of the coming confrontation with Fascism. But though he felt strongly enough about that to travel out to Spain to show solidarity with the Republic at the height of the Spanish Civil War in 1938, he wanted to preserve his own freedom as a freelance in the teeth of every storm, political and economic.

Spelling it "free lance" reminds us of the term's not particularly noble origins in mercenary warfare. Being a freelance is neither as noble nor as easy as some think. Rates for the job, in particular, seem to be declining—not something Horace had to worry about, once he had been granted his gilded independence with the gift of the Sabine Farm, the country estate in the Monti Lucretili given to him by Maecenas around 31 B.C. Later Horatian writers such as Pope, who in some ways modeled his entire writing career on Horace, both envied and criticized Horace for this. "Horace might keep his coach in Augustus' time, if he pleas'd, but I won't in the time of our Augustus," wrote Pope and Gay to their friend Swift in 1727. But a century earlier, Ben Jonson, who had more in common socially with Horace than most later Horatians, put Horace on the stage in his play *The Poetaster* to say "My soul is free as Caesar's."

Freedom always turns out to be more complicated than you think. There are signs in Horace's later work that the wonderful, shining freedom of the lyric poet, that bright target, luminous with the far-off light of ancient Greece, which he had aimed at and achieved with all his strength and sweetness, could have turned into another gilded cage. Being asked by Augustus to write the "Carmen Saeculare," an official festival hymn, was Horace's proudest public honor, but produced an unsatisfactory artistic compromise.

You might think that the achievement of the odes was enough, should be enough. But it wasn't enough for Horace. Both before and after the odes he wrote other kinds of poetry, surprisingly different and sometimes not like poetry at all. He even questioned the value of poetry. His *sermones* are usually translated as "satires" but they are not really like satires; they are more like conversations, examples of a free-flowing conversational poetry that looks forward to the twentieth century.

And then there are the two books of verse letters, or epistles. Here we find a completely different Horace. You could think of Yeats in his late poetry, especially in "The Circus Animals' Desertion," putting away his dazzling collection of masks, forced to start again from where everything starts, "the foul rag-and-bone shop of the heart."

Now we have an aging man, not particularly well, troubled by something, or a host of things. Once again you could think of Yeats, this time in "What Then?" Everything he wished for when young has come to pass. He has fulfilled his early promise, become a famous poet; he lives in the comfort and beauty of the Sabine Farm. But still he is not satisfied. "'What then?' sang Plato's ghost. 'What then?'"

This Horace is as much a philosopher as a poet. In the first epistle of Book 1 he speaks to Maecenas in a very different tone from the one he has used in the Odes. He sounds stern, almost truculent. He is going to give up poetry and devote himself to philosophy, the study of what is true and right.

But that is a sort of ruse, or feint. The epistles are poetry, but poetry of a different kind, more nakedly concerned with the questions of how to live, how to live well, how to conduct relationships with those you depend on for patronage while remaining free; how to be free in your mind.

Book 1 of the Epistles marks a turn: a turn toward philosophy, a turn away from the luxury of lyric, a turn from "dulce" to "utile."

This turn toward philosophy is one of the most interesting things about Horace, one of the things that draws me and has drawn so many others to him, but again it needs some explanation. First of all philosophy here is not an academic discipline. It is the study, which should concern all thinking human beings, of how to live and how to die.

This philosophy has much more in common with the contemporary practices of psychotherapy and psychoanalysis than with contemporary academic philosophy. Indeed the Greek philosopher Epicurus, in many ways Horace's mentor, had this to say: "What use is philosophy, unless it casts out suffering from the soul?"

Horace's concern with philosophy, like my own concern with psychotherapy, stems from personal feelings of dissatisfaction and distemper. Horace, who has come to be pictured as one of the smuggest writers who ever lived, can also sound like this: "What [do you say], when my mind is fighting with itself, spurns what it was desperately seeking, looks again for what it has just thrown away; when it changes like a tide, jangles against the equal temperament of life, pulls everything to pieces, builds it up again, tries to square the circle?"

In fact what Horace is doing in this philosophical, therapeutic poetry is immensely interesting and has still not been given its due. The fact that he is a poet first and a philosopher second (some of course would deny that he was a philosopher at all) allows him to be fundamentally human and inconsistent.

The hazard with philosophy is that it tends to elevate system above humanity. This was the trouble with Lucretius, the great Epicurean philosopher-poet whom Horace clearly admired but did not wish to emulate. *De rerum natura*, Lucretius's vast philosophical poem in six books of hexameters setting out the Epicurean system, is a magnificent achievement but it has one fundamental flaw. It failed to heal its own creator. According to St. Jérome, Lucretius was poisoned by a love potion and took his own life at the age of forty-four.

Another way of putting this is that Lucretius's *De rerum natura* is an immense monologue, or a vast lecture. Horace, especially in his later work, in the Odes and the Epistles, is fundamentally concerned with dialogue, with the therapeutic practice of friendship.

No poet I know of, in the entire history of poetry, has been more concerned with friendship. Poets, in fact, have often seemed rather self-obsessed, concerned above all with the strength and intensity and exquisiteness of their own feelings. Lyric poets might address their poems to a you, the beloved, but there is often the sense either that this you is not listening, or that he or she is a kind of mirror image of the poet's ego.

Horace is different. The characteristic form of his odes is the address to a friend, or a god or a bottle of wine or a spring. The vocative case is really meant; this is a true call to the other. The friends are real friends. The vocative implies a context, which is some kind of friendly conversation, over a bottle of wine, around the fire looking out at the winter view, or gazing out at the winter sea, not the poet wandering alone, close to despair, or tossing on his lonely bed in his garret as in Henry Wallis's Victorian painting *The Death of Chatterton*.

Perhaps Samuel Taylor Coleridge alone among the English Romantic poets was trying to do something similar when he wrote his Conversation poems. These uniquely touching poems could only arise in the context of friendship—the intense friendship between Coleridge and William and Dorothy Wordsworth—and when that context was broken, so too was the possibility of this kind of poetry.

In envisioning poetry as therapeutic dialogue and friendship, Horace was reaching far beyond his own time, perhaps into a time we have not yet attained. Close to the heart of the Odes, it seems to me, is Horace's attempt to cast out suffering from the soul of his friend and patron Maecenas.

The way Horace sets his poetry in the frame of friendship has also had a profound effect on all later poets' relationships with Horace. This odd idea of claiming Horace as a friend (not unique to me, as you will see) is not so peculiar when you consider the way Horace made his poetry profoundly companionable. Alongside my own developing friendship with Horace I will set stories and vignettes of so many others who have felt in a similar way.

Horace always starts with and comes back to what W. H. Auden, another Horatian, calls in his great poem "Musée des Beaux Arts" the "human position." Perhaps that makes him a poet-philosopher rather than a philosopher-poet. That means acknowledging the sheer thrownness (as Heidegger put it) of the human situation; we are always already embodied, thrown into this particular body we inhabit (in Horace's case short, prematurely gray, plump as a pint pot), this aging mortal body always already on its way toward death, toward that mysterious encounter in the underworld. Into this body and this temperament and character; in Horace's case quick to anger, quick to be appeased.

We do not float above the earth in some idealized space, the space of pure thought. We are of the earth, earthy; no one has reminded us of that, of its glory and sadness, more humanely and touchingly than Horace. Horace's earthiness is always localized. It has to do with place.

He and his friend Virgil and their predecessor Catullus deserve immortal glory, it seems to me, if for nothing else, then for this: for celebrating the particularity and beauty of place. Long before Wordsworth and the Romantics, they invented landscape in poetry.

They bring landscape down to earth. It is no longer mythical landscape that counts, but real particular places, that "corner," that little bit of land, with the woods and the never-failing stream, that matter so much to Horace.

Most famously of course it is the Sabine Farm, which has become a symbol to all subsequent poets of the good country life, what we might now call the sustainable life. The Sabine Farm has proved one of the most potent and enduring images in the whole of poetry, as potent and enduring as Wordsworth's lakes and mountains and his field of daffodils. And for this, Wordsworth, whom you might think an unlikely Horatian, loved Horace. You could even say that Horace's farm was a more enduring poetic symbol than Wordsworth's lakes and hills and daffodils, because it incorporates man into nature.

The Sabine Farm's appeal is not just to poets: all those who retreat to restored farmhouses in Provence or Tuscany are consciously or unconsciously following Horace. But you don't need to abscond to some Arcadian idyll; anywhere in any place, in the city or the country or the edgelands between, you can watch the sunlight on the garden, as MacNeice called it in his most Horatian lyric.

The farm was not large, Horace tells us, but it had the essentials: some woodland, a spring that never failed, a plentiful supply of fruit, oaks to provide shade for the cattle. From one of his most deeply felt odes, in which he speaks of serving Maecenas an ordinary Sabine wine he himself had sealed in Greek jars, we can deduce that the farm possessed vines; in any case the vine and its product, wine, is the essential agricultural symbol of Horace's poetry.

You could say there is nothing more central to Horace's poetry, and philosophy, than wine. Wine comes again and again in the Odes, and the Satires and the Epistles, as a master symbol that gathers much of the meaning of the poetry. The centrality of wine often passes relatively unnoticed, or is overlooked because "it is just a convention" or because wine is surely not serious as a subject.

The prominence of wine in Horace's poetry was not overlooked by me, for good and obvious reasons. I was the son of a wine merchant; I grew up among bottles and boxes of the restorative fluid. Wine was central to our family economy and to my father's philosophy. Wine was also what drew me to Horace in the first place, what forged a connection I couldn't miss. Though there was much I couldn't and didn't understand about Horace, I immediately understood what he felt and expressed about wine, how he grasped wine's deeper power even as he also relished different vintages and crus as a Roman connoisseur.

Horace's relation to wine in his poetry—looking back to wine's divine origins in ancient Greece, and forward to wine's status as a plutocrat's plaything—gave me the key to the connection between his time and our time, even between him and me.

Just before he issues his most famous injunction, "Carpe diem" (usually translated as "Seize the day" but in my view better rendered as "Taste the day"), Horace instructs his interlocutor, or girlfriend, or muse, with the beautiful Greek name Leuconoe, to "be wise, and strain the wine." They go together, the wisdom, the wine, the enjoyment of the day; the wisdom that does not strain to know too much, to know what cannot be known; the wisdom that is content to live in the radical uncertainty of the mortal present.

But I am getting ahead of myself. I need to retrace my steps, as far as possible with those of Horace, in his different, earlier world.

Three

The Soul of Wine

Wine was my first strong link with Horace. Because Horace loved wine, I overcame my suspicions of him, my feeling that he might be a propagandist, or a poet who avoided strong emotion; to put it in Wodehousian terms, anyone who understood wine so well must be fundamentally a good egg.

In one way my connection with wine was even stronger and earlier than Horace's; wine was close to the center of our family's life and our family economy: the house where I was born sits on top of a wine cellar, a cellar where my wine merchant father's most precious bottles were stored. When Horace talked about bringing out a special jar from the cellar, I didn't need any scholarly explanation; I understood it in my bones.

Wine has been not just a business for my father but a passion, a way of life and a fulfillment. From the moment he decided, while waiting for a commuter train one morning, to give up a career in advertising and embark on the much riskier venture of setting up as an independent wine merchant, he had found his way. The business would quite quickly move from a small shop in Somerset, where my father for a few years spent his weekdays, back to our house, and assorted outbuildings on a nearby farm that he rented for storage.

For as long as I can remember, not just the cellar but the house has been benignly cluttered with wooden cases and cardboard boxes packed with wine; with individual bottles left on top of cupboards; with all sorts of special wineglasses and corkscrews and decanters; with labels soaked off bottles and stuck on walls as decorations. Wine has in some sense permeated the whole place.

This wonderful and mysterious paraphernalia permeated my soul also, as a dimension of being, parallel to other dimensions such as golf, music, and photography, all passions of my father and all to be imparted to me. Each had its own vocabulary, its sensual side (the smells, tastes, feel, sounds, look), its intellectual and emotional dimension. Wine was not just a delicious substance with wonderful powers, but a way of communicating, a discourse. From the beginning I was brought up to understand that wine was not only something to drink but something to appreciate and to discuss.

A lot of the conversation around my parents' dining table centered on wine, and I suppose quite early on I gathered that talking about wine could be a way of talking about other things. Of course it all started to become infinitely more interesting when I was allowed to taste my first drops.

The first wine I can remember tasting and discussing with my father was a German Riesling from the tiny Ruwer valley with the ringing name of Maximin Grünhäuser Herrenberg Riesling Spätlese. It had been vintaged in the year of my birth, 1958. I was eight years old; the green-tingling fresh taste of this fine, subtle, crisp wine with a hint of sweetness and a prickle of carbon dioxide captivated me as much as the beautiful label, a colored engraving of the hillside vineyard and elegant manor house that I would one day visit.

My wine education continued precociously. At age thirteen I attended a lunch at the headquarters of a champagne company outside Reims at which a different champagne was served with each course. I think there were five or six courses; somewhat anxious parental glances were cast in my direction after the fourth or fifth; and I was rather disappointed not to be offered a glass of the Marc de Champagne that came at the end.

By my midteens I was accompanying my father on wine-tasting trips to France and Germany. At some point I had begun to enjoy and appreciate red wines and to learn the names and classifications of the leading wines of Bordeaux and Burgundy. The difference between the two fascinated me: Bordeaux with its more upright bottles, with a certain firmness or classical structure; Burgundy with its sloping bottles, perfumed, sensuous, elusive.

At fifteen I drove with my father down to Burgundy, where we sampled wines made by small, artisanal growers in their cold, richly smelling cellars. These wines, from the Côte Chalonnaise villages of Rully, Mercurey, and Givry, were then little known and some were rustic: one consignment of Rully that we shipped back began to referment in the summer, the bottles turning cloudy and in some cases popping their corks.

My father's favorite wine country was Germany. His love affair with wine had begun in unlikely circumstances. Serving in the Army of Occupation in the devastated remains of Hamburg in 1945–46, he had come across German Riesling; the experience also convinced him of the immorality of the Allied policy of area bombing. Perhaps in reaction to all that, and to the blimpish militarism of the class in which he had been brought up, my father became a Germanophile: an enthusiast for all aspects of German culture and a specialist importer of fine German wine.

We made more tasting trips to Germany than to any other country, driving through Belgium and Luxembourg before hitting the German border near the ancient Roman town of Trier. The Porta Nigra, or black gate, of the Roman city founded in 16 B.C. (eight years before Horace died) as Augusta Treverorum had survived miraculously intact while most of the rest of the city had been bombed and then rebuilt, with a perfection I found faintly eerie.

The gate was not the only Roman survivor; the vertiginously steep hand-tended vineyards lining the valley of the Mosel represented an extraordinary cultural continuity: nearly two thousand years of viticulture, defying the vicissitudes of history and the remark of Pliny the Elder that "vineyards, like states, have their rise, their greatness, and their fall."

I would find out later that not all vineyards look the same. The immaculately groomed crus of the Médoc are as regular and smooth as a pin-striped suit, and about as interesting. In Châteauneuf-du-Pape I saw vines like old gnarled hands protrude through huge white pebbles. Some of the mechanically pruned vineyards of southern Australia give the impression of having been attacked by vandals. But the vineyards of the Mosel glow like a medieval tapestry; they look as if they have been stitched to the hillside.

Just as much as in France, wine in this historic part of Germany seemed like a deep and serious facet of culture, not an alcoholic drink to be manufactured as cheaply and efficiently as possible. The estates whose wines we tasted in and around Trier had in some cases belonged to monasteries or other religious entities; one still formed part of the patrimony of an ancient grammar school, the Friedrich Wilhelm Gymnasium, the school where Karl Marx received his secondary education; others belonged to the German state. Even the private estates seemed to be cared for with an almost religious devotion.

The directors of these estates were men of quasi-monastic mien, intensely serious and apparently less interested in commerce than discussing the particular characteristics of wines from different vineyards harvested at different degrees of ripeness. The names could not have been further removed from the world of commercial branding; rather than being short, simple, and easy to memorize, they were Byzantine in their complexity. To call a wine something like Eitelsbacher Karthäuserhofberg Riesling Spätlese 1976 was to display a magnificent disregard for easy popularity. A tasting at an estate such as the Friedrich Wilhelm Gymnasium or the Bischöfliche Weingüter or the legendary J. J. Prüm was more like an academic seminar than an exercise in salesmanship.

At his elegant nineteenth-century villa on the riverfront in Wehlen, the eccentric Manfred Prüm would conduct tastings in his own inimitable way. No question, as with other estates, of sampling a range of wines from the latest vintage: no, Manfred would select only vintages, and wines, that he believed were ready to be tasted on that particular day. On one occasion, I remember, he would only show wines from the unfashionable 1977 vintage. On the occasions my father and I visited him he showed no interest in selling anything. In some ways Manfred was a pioneer of the slow movement, the worldwide cultural shift toward a steadier tempo of living; his idiosyncratic way of presenting only wines that had reached a certain maturity was a rebuke to overhurried times. It also meant, I imagine, that he had to keep an enormous number of bottles maturing in his cellars—a practice that no accountant would consider rational.

On those trips to Germany, now that I look back, I imbibed the essential aspects of a deep and serious wine culture. Showiness and pretension were absent. Before the First World War, the finest German wines had been among the most sought-after and expensive in the world; at a Christie's auction in 1877, for instance, a Steinberger 1857, from one of the Rhine's best vineyards, sold for the same price, ninety shillings a dozen, as the celebrated 1865 vintage of Château Lafite. Schloss Johannisberg 1862, another top Rhine wine, was forty shillings a dozen more.

After the Second World War, things had changed. The emphasis in German wine-making shifted from quality to quantity: industrial quantities of Liebfraumilch were produced, vineyard names were corrupted by ill-conceived wine laws, and the reputation of German wines plummeted.

The quality-conscious growers my father and I visited were

battling against the odds to restore the reputation of German wine, for the most part in an essentially modest way. German wine and wine-making had a charm, born of passionate dedication to particular plots of land, that I also would find in Burgundy and a few other favored corners of the earth. This wine land of winding river valleys with slopes either planted with vines or dense with wild cherry, beech, and oak was extraordinarily beautiful. One May night, staying in the bucolic valley of the river Nahe, I was kept awake by an impassioned nightingale.

Wine quite naturally for me became part of education, of life, of culture—as much as music or literature. But wine was different in its earthiness, in the way it combined the humdrum and the spiritual.

I got to know wine's humdrum side during one of my university summer vacations, when I went to do what the French call a *stage* at the famous Rhône valley wine firm of Paul Jaboulet Aîné. I knew, from tasting the wines with my father, who included the Jaboulet wines on his list, that the company made one of the northern Rhône's, and perhaps the world's, greatest wines, the magnificent Hermitage La Chapelle from Jaboulet's own vineyards. In fact my father had opened a stray bottle of the famous 1961 vintage one Christmas lunch, a wine of astonishing wild, tarry intensity; the Jaboulet domaine also included a Crozes-Hermitage, Domaine de Thalabert, far better than most of the often rather dull wines of that appellation.

What I had not experienced was the laborious business of assembling cardboard cases and other mechanical work in the chai, with the wild-eyed brother of the smooth managing director behaving like an ancient Roman slave driver. Far from romantic, I found the grinding monotony of the work, the clanking of the bottling line, the complete lack of intellectual and emotional stimulation, pretty dispiriting. And the town of Tain-l'Hermitage, despite its vineyard-clad hills and elegant suspension bridge over the Rhône, was southern provincial France at its most dustily hidebound and inert.

I expect I was an annoyingly vague and rarefied youth; I endured one of the loneliest months of my life, staying in a hotel positioned directly above one of France's busiest *routes nationales*, eating meals on my own in the hotel restaurant (the company provided *pension complète*), each one accompanied by a quarter liter of house red, somewhat morosely reading novels by Stendhal. This reading only confirmed my sense of being a misunderstood sensitive spirit in a world of crude (Stendhal's word was *grossier*) calculation, industry, and commerce.

I was delighted to be invited one weekend to visit a French family with a wine farm in the Beaujolais country; there were two svelte and soignée daughters I had met the previous summer through friends in my home village in the Chilterns. "Why do you want to go to Beaujolais?" asked one of my coworkers in the Jaboulet chai, as I set off on the bus to Villefranche-sur-Saône. "Isn't our wine good enough for you?" Nothing developed with either of the daughters; in fact my main memory is of some complicated etiquette regarding table napkins that I never mastered.

Back at university in England, I found myself getting involved with the Cambridge University Wine and Food Society, and quite quickly graduating to the tasting team. We took our training reasonably seriously, but not grimly so, meeting in a don's room to sample a half dozen wines, to get a grounding in the major European wine styles (the New World was still considered too new).

Two years running, I managed to win the individual prize in the Oxford versus Cambridge blind tasting competition, the so-called bibbers' boat race, beating fellow contestants who included the formidable ginger-haired brother-and-sister combination of Arabella and Jasper Morris, both of whom would end up as Masters of Wine. I felt quite proud to be in a line that included the distinguished wine writers and broadcasters Jancis Robinson, Oz Clarke, and Charles Metcalfe. But I suppose I'd had a head start.

Wine came to my rescue more than once in the difficult years after leaving university and beginning to make my way in the world. Having given up my PhD, and got bogged down in attempts to write short stories in the small room at the top of my parents' house, I landed a job working as wine controller at the Tate Gallery restaurant.

This must have been one of the cushiest jobs ever devised; the actual supervision of stock was done by the control freak of a restaurant manager, the formidably built Miss Hayward, while wine service was in the hands of a tightly knit band of waitresses, who did not want any outsider intruding on their lucrative patch. I was only rarely called on to do any work, on occasions when guests had a complaint or a query. A furious American accused me of having "de-aged" his bottle of Bordeaux by ten years by serving it in a decanter; I explained that it was our normal practice to decant older vintages of Bordeaux, to separate the clear wine from the sediment.

I left the Tate after little more than a month, because my father got wind of a possible job for me as a junior expert at Christie's wine department, working under the charismatic and talented wine auctioneer and wine writer Michael Broadbent. It could have been the start of a career, I suppose, but I never felt truly happy or in my element at Christie's. Wine auctioneering, for all its veneer of class, turned out to be another pretty humdrum occupation—though not for Michael Broadbent, who had created a small niche of glamour for himself as a jet-setting wine celebrity, while everybody else in the office toiled in near Dickensian conditions.

To be fair, Broadbent held regular tastings in the office. In the early 1980s there were still country house cellars in Britain where remarkable collections of old classic wine lurked, forgotten or ignored by absentminded owners.

One day several cases of Château Margaux from the great 1893, 1899, and 1900 vintages arrived in the office. They had lain undisturbed in a northern Irish cellar for the entire course of the twentieth century; they had rested peacefully, in their dreamless sleep, through the Irish Civil War and two World Wars, through the Bolshevik Revolution and the Chinese Revolution, the Korean War and the Vietman War; they had been undisturbed by the invention of the contraceptive pill and the atomic bomb.

Normally, of course, the bottles of fine old wines we auctioned could be described only from the outside, with notes on the level of wine in the bottle, the condition of the label, and so on. But in this case, and by agreement with the owners, Broadbent had arranged that one or two bottles of each vintage should be opened and tasted; a tasting note would carry more weight than any description. We were allowed to taste too; all three vintages of Margaux, still in their original wrapping paper, were deep red in color, with exquisite bouquets and vigorous fruit, the ironlike flavor of mature Cabernet Sauvignon, as healthy as a vigorous octogenarian. It was a moment of magic, an example of wine's uniquely intimate companionship with human life; a Horatian moment.

I never adapted either to office life or to the ethos of Christie's. I decided that wearing a pin-striped suit and ingratiating myself before aristocrats and tycoons was not my cup of tea. My greatest pleasures, in fact, were those of mild, verging on moderate, subversion.

Michael Broadbent, despite well-founded suspicions about my commitment and attitude toward the job, respected my tasting ability and the knack I quickly picked up of writing short tasting notes in the Broadbent style. While cataloging a sale of finest and rarest wines in his absence, I came across a lot described as consisting of "six bottles of Dr Rutland's Invalid Port." This seemed to invite a fictitious note, so I added "prescribed for

Sir Winston Churchill during the Second World War as a tonic." To my surprise, this note made it through into the printed version of the catalog; the lot was purchased by Bill Baker of Reid Wines, one of the funniest men in the wine trade, who reproduced my note in his own catalog. Years later, not long before his untimely death, I told him about the deception, and he laughed his fruity laugh. "We had it on the list for years. Nothing would shift it."

More seriously subversive was a conversation I had with the *Evening Standard*'s "Londoner's Diary" about the sale of some wines from the cellar of Princess Margaret. I described them, accurately but unflatteringly, as "a medley of old bin-ends" and said I was surprised Her Royal Highness wanted to put her name to such an undistinguished collection. Of course, the diarist printed my remarks, which were truthful but unflattering in the extreme, and unbelievably undiplomatic.

Even more oddly, my boss did not trace the remarks back to me; perhaps he assumed he had made them himself, in a fit of absentminded honesty; in any case, he composed a letter of apology and cycled over to Kensington Palace to deliver it in person.

Obviously, I was skating on thin ice; quite angry also, and unfulfilled. Wine was keeping me afloat but it was not satisfying my dreams. I needed a new way of relating to it. Stifled by an excessively worldly, snobbish relationship with wine, I needed to attain to its poetry.

Horace has been accused, by the mayor of London and perceptive Horatian Boris Johnson, of being a typical nouveau riche wine snob. Perhaps he was, in a way, but he was also a scourge of wine snobs, an anti–wine snob.

I think Horace was more than a wine snob; he was a true connoisseur, who knew and cared about wine's intimate secrets, the different crus and vintages, which mattered as much to the Romans as they do to us. But he was also something of a vintner, a man who personally drew off his own country wine from its fermenting tubs or vessels and siphoned it into amphorae that he sealed with pitch. He was a wine lover, who saw beyond wine as a status symbol to the divine power of wine as a consoler and inspirer of humanity.

Reading Horace's odes, you cannot fail to notice how frequently the poet mentions wine. It is probably harder to find a poem that does not include a reference to wine than one that does. And dry scholarly talk of a Greek tradition of drinking songs hardly does justice to Horace's unmistakably intense and serious interest in wine.

Wine is many things in Horace's poetry. It is a topic, a poetic theme, a symbol. It has a social dimension, a literary dimension, but also a spiritual dimension.

Wine is obviously a talking point, a topic of conversation, in Horace's society. The Romans cared about wine; it was an important part of their economy. Or perhaps it would be more accurate to say that Italians have always cared about wine. The Romans, using an old Greek word, called southern Italy Oenotria, the land of wine; the Greek word draws attention to the way Greek colonial settlers in southern Italy brought with them the vine and their own wine culture, but in its application reminds us that Italy is still better endowed for wine production than any other European country. Certainly better than Greece, where slopes are often too harsh. Arguably better than France, which would like to think of itself as the land of the vine but where, except in the deep south, the practice of chaptalization (adding sugar to fermenting must) shows that the weather is not always hot enough to ripen grapes optimally.

Italy was and remains wine's wonderland. Wine was drunk by all classes in Roman times. At Pompeii you can see the ruins of 118 wine bars or restaurants. Hedone, the hostess of one of them, says to her clients, "You can drink here for one as; if you pay double you can have better wine, but if you pay four you can have Falernian." This shows that the Romans already had quite a sophisticated hierarchy of vineyards and what the French would call appellations.

The Roman hierarchy of Italian wine was different from to-day's, which favors the northern province of Piedmont and the north-central province of Tuscany. The majority of the Italian wines the Romans prized most came from the south, from Campania, which still produces some exceptional wines from volcanic soils. These were Falernian (definitely the premier grand cru); also Caecuban, Calenian, Setine, Statanian. Certain quite highly prized wines came from Latium, especially Massic, Formian, and Alban.

How good were these Roman wines, or how good did they taste? The sections on viticulture in Cato's *De agri cultura* (c. 160 B.C.), Varro's *Rerum rusticarum* (37 B.C.), Pliny's *Natural History*, and, above all and the jewel of Roman farming handbooks, Columella's *De re rustica* (c. A.D. 50) show that the Romans were expert and discriminating wine growers and winemakers. They knew, for example, how important vineyard location was; they paid attention to pruning, the stripping of excess leaves, and the date of harvesting; Columella stresses the necessity of hygiene in the winery.

Above all, there is the consistent evidence of the amazing aging potential of Roman wines. Decanted into pottery jars and sealed with pitch, Roman wines could last longer, and were regularly drunk at an older age, than most modern ones. Columella states that "almost every wine has the property of acquiring excellence with age"—something you certainly could not say about modern wines. Sabine, the kind of wine Horace produced on his own farm and not highly prized, was considered ready for drinking after seven to ten years. Your average Frascati, the modern white wine of the Alban hills, fifteen miles or so to the south, is usually past its best by the age of three.

So wine is a talking point, and in particular it is something for Horace to talk about with the most important person in his life, his friend and patron Maecenas:

VILE POTABIS (ODES 1.20)

Just the basic plonk, in standard tumblers,
The local Sabine wine is what you'll get
From me Maecenas—but my own: a jar
Of home-brew I laid up and sealed

The day, my friend, you had your triumph:
When the applause was thunderous, grateful
Romans acknowledging what you'd done,
The happy echo ringing round seven hills.

Then you drank the best Brunello, without doubt;
But as I say you'll get no grands crus here,
Just what I grow in my own shady valley
Here, in the corner that you blessed me with.

As usual with Horace, the apparently simple, almost casual poem is infinitely rich in meanings. The best discussion of this poem I know, by the sympathetic Horace scholar David West, finds a subtle compliment paid by Horace to his patron and friend in almost every word of the poem.

The very first word of the poem, "vile" in Latin, which I have translated as "basic plonk," pays an oblique sort of compliment. It does credit to the grand Maecenas, who is used to, as we see from the last stanza, the grandest of grands crus, that he will come and drink country wine with his poet friend; that he prizes friendship above status.

Horace is not as rich and grand as Maecenas. That is blindingly obvious. But he is his own man; and the way the poet expresses that is by saying that this unpretentious, ordinary country wine from his own estate is one he personally bottled, or drew off into amphorae and sealed with pitch. The most powerful word in the whole poem is "myself," "ipse" in Latin.

A Sabine wine is nothing to boast about. According to Galen, Sabine was the thinnest of all Italian wines (if you can find any, it is probably not all that much better today). This humble vino locale bears no comparison to Falernian or Formian, celebrated, expensive wines from farther south (which I have translated as Brunello, the top Tuscan wine today). But the wine is of Horace's own production and comes from the place, the Sabine Farm given to him by Maecenas, that he loves above all others.

This humble wine stands for the humble poet, the freedman's son, and beyond that for the poetry this man wrote, which was a kind of transformation of humility into eternity.

Horace knew something that wine snobs often forget, that there are things even more important than wine, or at least wine connoisseurship. Some of my most sterile social evenings have been lubricated with magnificent vintages, which died somewhere between the glass and the mouth because the right spirit needed to appreciate them was absent.

Friendship and warmth count for more, in the end, than the label on the bottle. The triumph that Horace refers to in this poem seems to have marked Maecenas's recovery from serious illness. The anniversary wine is Horace's way of showing his appreciation, even his love; not among the ranks of grand Roman senators and knights, but well away from the "smoke and din and opulence," in the secluded valley among the hills.

I do like to think, though, that Horace's "vile Sabinum" was rather better than he implies; that he put considerable care into the production of this unpretentious country wine and ended up with something better than the modest appellation—something that may not have been big and powerful but was at least honest, speaking in its own accent. Indeed as Pliny the Elder said: "Today even the wealthiest do not drink natural wines. So dishonest has the trade become that wines are sold on names alone; new vintages are adulterated as soon as they enter the vats. So, in a strange twist, the less reputed a wine is, the more likely it is to be authentic."

For all his commitment to country simplicity, Horace obviously knew his top vineyards, and enjoyed his Caecuban and Falernian and Formian with the best of them. He mentions these wines, the grands crus of the Roman world, quite frequently—though often ironically. He even seems to have kept some of them in his cellar, as the next poem shows.

But I think he was even more aware and appreciative of vintages than of crus. Vintages, after all, bring in the dimension of time; of birth, aging, and death, which wine has in common with human beings.

O NATA MECUM (ODES 3.21)

Your time is up, my faithful aged
Margaux, contemporary, my twin—
Just think of it, you were vintaged
The year of Supermac's shameless spin,
That "you've never had it so good" guff—
Oh come, descend: old friend
Jim has called for smoother stuff.

Heaven knows what havoc or ferment—
What vehement argument
Or crazy love obsession
Or merciful slumping
Into snores you have in store.

Though philosophically inclined
And aptest to peruse
Abstruser tomes by Plato

I know my friend will not refuse
A little tipple of the warming kind
Not scorned by stern old Cato.

In vino veritas, they say; you,
Venerable vintage, have the subtle knack
Of mellowing tough nuts; such a dusty
Bottle can unlock from the most crusty
The best-kept secret and release the craic.

And that's not all; you can restore
To a desperate mind the balm of hope;
Give strength and sustenance to the poor
Man faced with all the aftermath of war;
One wee dram and he'll feel potent as a pope.

Your presence brings diviner traces—
Goatlike Bacchus and the gorgeous Venus,
If she's willing, and the gang of Graces,
So slow to untie their virgins' girdles,
All dance around us while we drink till dawn.

This glorious ode has in general flummoxed commentators. Most of them seem fixated on its parodic elements and assume that Horace is being daringly irreverent in addressing an ode to a wine jar (rather than a god, let's say).

I'm sure there's an element of parody, but only those with a puritan or teetotal disdain for the truth and beauty of wine could underestimate this poem.

Apparently the greatest of all Horace scholars, Eduard Fraenkel, Professor of Latin at Oxford from 1935 to 1953, who, like me, was the son of a wine merchant, spoke movingly about these lines to his students at Oxford. But even he, rather strangely, does not mention them at all in his tome on Horace.

This ode, significantly longer than "Vile potabis," is a kind of summation of Horace's view of wine. For a start it is intensely personal and concerned with the cycles of birth and death that link humanity and wine, and make it such a potent poetic symbol. The first three words of the ode in Latin are "O nata mecum," which mean "O born with me." He addresses this particular wine jar as his twin. He gives it human, even transhuman force. Nothing could be further from the view of wine as a fancy accessory or a status symbol.

And then the second thing: wine is always for Horace intimately linked with friendship. You feel the friendship in this case is a particularly close one. Marcus Valerius Messalla Corvinus, the addressee of this ode, was an old friend of Horace's, and a comrade-in-arms on the field of Philippi, who later went on to achieve military distinction and to become consul. Apparently he had no taste for political power and preferred his privacy. It's interesting that whereas Maecenas gets just the local vino locale, Messalla Corvinus is honored with one of the best bottles in Horace's collection.

Wine is not just cozy; it has unpredictable powers. It is linked to some of the most dangerous gods. Wine fosters friendship, but it is also a loosener; it releases the mind from its shackles, of reserve or excessive reason.

This can take the drinker into perilous realms, as we will see from the next poem, but overwhelmingly Horace's view of wine is positive. He sees it as one of the greatest helpers of humanity. Horace's own humanity, his sympathy with the sufferings of his fellow beings, comes out beautifully here. Wine does not just lift mood—no small thing, especially to anyone prone to depression—but can transcend social division.

Wine is human and mortal; it is born and it dies, in the *Liebestod* of libation, or as it meets human lips and disappears down human gullets. But, as the end of the ode makes clear, it has connections with immortality.

One of the main reasons Horace invokes wine so much in his poetry is that wine and poetry are intimately and profoundly linked. Drinking inspires and poetry is the product of inspiration.

Wine and poetry are quite alike in their natures and their effects. Both are the result of a sort of alchemy: ordinary common or garden words, the rough currency of conversation, are transformed in poetry into immortal phrases and lines. The mysteries of fermentation and aging turn grape juice, a fairly unmagical substance, into something that can live as long as a human being, and share human complexity. Above all, wine and poetry share a god.

QUO ME BACCHE (ODES 3.25)

Where are you rushing me off to, Wine God?
I am being driven wild, into the woods,
Into a troll's cave, I'm inspired.

There's something absolutely fresh,
Which no one has ever written before,
A new kind of poetry, the poetry of peace.

I'm like a Bacchant, one of your wild ones,
Silent upon a Greek peak, high above Hebron,
Looking out over a frozen landscape,

And the Rhodope, at the very bounds
Of civilization, and beyond; because I too
Like to stray off-piste, into empty woods.

O you who have power over river spirits
And women who uproot trees with bare hands,
Full of you I will speak grand things,

My words will soar, O Lord of the Wine Press,
And they will not die; I am drinking deep,
Taking the risk, binding my brow with vine shoots.

The poem is about inspiration. Horace is addressing his master
inspirer, not just the god who presides over the wine press and
the mystery of fermentation, but the one who transports him to
new mental realms ("mente nova"), which represent poetic power
and invention. The imagery of the poem is far from homely: Horace imagines being rushed off his feet into wild territory, the
river valleys and mountains of northern Greece, on the borders
of civilization, associated with the Bacchants, those intoxicated
female followers of the wine god who in Euripides's *Bacchae*
tear men limb from limb.

Poetry and wine are liminal things. They live on the border-
lands between the wild and the civilized, between reason and
irrationality. Their territory is the unplanned, the unexpected,
the pathless (a word Horace particularly liked). Both have the
potential for danger—for mad love affairs, fights, violence. Both
speak to our need for the wild, as well as the civilized, the irra-
tional as well as the rational. Horace, famous for moderation,
also said "to revel wildly is my delight." The so-called wine snob
saw that wine was not just vino, something you glug in a bar, but
vino divino, our connection with the divine.

This was something the Spanish philosopher José Ortega y
Gasset remembered as he strolled through the galleries of the
Museo del Prado one summer afternoon. Ortega paused in front
of three wine-soaked paintings, Titian's *Bacchanal*, Poussin's
Bacchanal, and Velázquez's *Drunkards*.

Looking at the first two paintings, set in a mythical, classical
world, Ortega was led to reflect on the difference between the
modern age and the classical era that had inspired the paintings.
Scientific materialism had shattered the great maternal quarry

of Nature into a chaos of fragments: "We possess," says Ortega with Nietzschean irony, "the rubble of life." Instead of an organic unity, modern man lives in a disarticulated world of boxes. But for ancient man, not just the endless specialisms but the primary distinction between physical and spiritual matters did not exist. Ancient man saw wine as something elemental; the sun-swollen berries of the vine "condensed an astonishing force which gave power to humans and animals and led them to a better life."

Wine connects: seized by Bacchus the wine god, we feel as if "invisible fingers were weaving our being into the earth, the sea, the air, the sky; as if the world were a tapestry and we ourselves figures in that tapestry and the threads forming our breasts extended beyond it and became consubstantial with that radiant cloud." Wine gives us those sublime moments when we "seem to coincide with all the universe."

Well, you might say, so many a drunk has imagined. But the deep truth in Ortega's suggestive remarks, which could just as well be a commentary on Horace, stand as a rebuke to much of the contemporary discourse on wine, to a deadly way of approaching and writing about the subject.

Some years after my time at Christie's, I became a wine writer. I was lucky; I fell into it, as into so many things. Well, not entirely lucky, because I knew my stuff and had been trained from an early age. But my luck was that my decision to embark on freelance wine writing coincided with a dramatic boom in wine consumption; and not only the appetite for drinking wine was growing but also the appetite for reading and learning about it.

This enviable profession took me to many beautiful places and brought me into contact with devoted artisanal producers. Talk of the spirituality and grace of wine made sense in the cold cellars of Vougeot in Burgundy, where the Grivots made wine from plots originally planted by Cistercian monks.

In the Portuguese Alentejo I saw wines still being fermented in terra cotta amphorae, in the old Roman way—and very good they were. Later I came across an unusual Italian vintner, Josko Gravner, who has come back to Roman methods of fermentation after trying every modern way. He truly believes that the most important texts written on viticulture are those composed two thousand years ago by Cato, Varro, Columella, and Pliny.

In the magnificent vaulted bodegas of Jerez and Sanlúcar de Barrameda in the far south of Spain I had fascinating conversations with the educators of those wines, who believed that every barrel had a distinct character.

I trod grapes in the troughs called *lagares* in a small quinta in a wild valley of a tributary of the river Douro, participating in a ritual, complete with accordion playing and dancing, that might not have seemed foreign to Horace.

Farther afield I admired the frontiersman spirit and the balance between the wild and the civilized you can find in certain wine estates in California, in the hills framing the Napa Valley, home of grotesque architectural excesses as well as fine wine.

Increasingly I felt that as the breadth of wines being offered was widening, the conversation was narrowing. As in other areas, the faith in technology, and in numbers, as the panacea for everything had not necessarily delivered a golden age of wine, or of wine writing. Many fewer wines with obvious faults were produced than in earlier times, no doubt, but too many wines were coming to taste alike. Technology had not put an end to the abuses against which Columella spoke with such feeling nearly two thousand years ago:

> Why then is [viticulture] in so great disreputation?
> Graecinus says, that it is not from its own fault, but from
> men's: first, because nobody gives diligence in examin-
> ing and trying the plants; and therefore most men plant
> vineyards of the worst kind. Then they don't cherish and
> nourish them, after they are planted, in such a manner,
> that they may grow strong, and shoot up, before they are

parched and burnt up with the heat; but if peradventure they grow up, they cultivate them negligently. Now, from the very beginning, they think, that it is of no importance what place they plant; yea, they even pick out the very worst part of their lands, as if that ground, which can bear no other thing, were only the fittest for this stem . . . Most people indeed are mighty intent upon having as much fruit for the present as is possible, and make no provision for the time to come; but, as if they lived altogether from hand to mouth, and had only regard for the present time, they so force the vines, and load them with so many fruit-bearing branches, that they have no regard for the interest of their posterity.

Obstinate perhaps, I did not wish to provide merely a consumer service, offering guidance on "best buys," but to speak of wine as part of culture and history, to delve into its profound connection with the place of its birth, the ways of doing and talking about things practiced by its makers and their ancestors.

The profession of wine grower and winemaker has come to seem to me as much philosophical as agricultural: a reflection of a thoughtful individual's view of the world and especially of nature. This obviously demands a different kind of wine writing from the one that gives pride of place to numerical ratings.

Four

Among the Centurions' Sons

I did not always get on with Horace. Toiling in the classroom at Eton College (which I had entered as a King's Scholar at age twelve, at a time when classics was still the dominant discipline in the lower half of the school), I had first been captivated by a very different Roman poet.

We were introduced to Latin verse through a small volume called *A First Book of Latin Poetry*, by H. W. Flewett and W.E.P. Pantin. Flewett and Pantin (one of those pairings destined for a certain immortality, like Tate & Lyle or Crosse & Blackwell) were both masters of the Special Form at St. Paul's School, and brought out their little book for the first time in 1943, just as the fortunes of the Second World War were turning.

Their "Personal Note to the Reader" begins in chilling fashion: "Everyone knows of the schoolmaster who, when laying on hard with the cane, says smugly between the whacks, 'This hurts me, my boy, more than it hurts you.'" Not much seems to have changed since the time of Horace and his stern teacher, Orbilius, whose nickname was "the flogger" and who inculcated in Horace the virtues of rugged antique Latin verse, the hexamaters of Ennius and Naevius. Horace never forgot them, but in his own aesthetic tempered their stark strength with Greek sophistication.

Flewett and Pantin became identified in my mind with my first Latin teacher, Mr. Needham at Farleigh House Preparatory

School, a Catholic boarding establishment that I attended from age eight to twelve. Mr. Needham, in his unvarying uniform of corduroy trousers and tweed jacket, with a collection of Parker pens filled with different-colored inks hooked on the inside pocket, was a crusty bachelor from the north of England, a supporter of the eternally unfashionable Lincoln City football club. He was not a smooth or charming man, but I greatly preferred him to our insincere headmaster, who had one manner with the parents and quite another with the boys.

Sometimes I came across Mr. Needham outside the classroom, practicing Handel's "Harmonious Blacksmith" variations with the same dogged determination he applied to everything. This seemed difficult music to me (as I was just starting to learn simple classical pieces), thick with demisemiquavers, but he was far too honest to claim to be a good pianist. Beneath it all I detected a rigorous search for beauty.

So I knew that Flewett and Pantin really did mean it when they said "this book is intended for your enjoyment." They even mention pleasure and delight. In the same note the crusty duo compare learning how to enjoy Latin poetry with learning how to enjoy fishing for trout. Comically true to type perhaps, but also genuine and quite unusual.

It was unusual because enjoyment and classics did not seem natural bedfellows. Having brought enjoyment, pleasure, and delight into the picture, Flewett and Pantin, as if embarrassed by what they have just done, attempt to banish them again. "As a great man—who was also a great trout-fisherman and a great lover of poetry, once wisely said, when writing on his favourite pastime—'nothing is more difficult than to convey any strong impression of pleasure,' and we cannot hope to make you understand what we have felt."

They are speaking about an intense delight that cannot really be communicated; that has to be hidden beneath layers of crustiness, dressed in the deceptive uniform of tweed jacket and corduroy trousers. But that intense enjoyment, pleasure, delight, is the heart of the matter. It is what makes the whole laborious, dogged business of learning the ancient language, all its intricacies of grammar and metrics, or piano playing, with its tricky fingerings and rhythms, worth the candle. Beneath their pedantic appearance, Flewett and Pantin are relayers of delight, wanting to hand down to the next generation a possibility of profound enjoyment.

The key to it all was, and is, the last word in the title of their little book, "poetry." And the poet who shone most brightly from their anthology, far eclipsing Horace, was his Republican predecessor Catullus.

The crusty duo were shrewd in starting off their selection with a generous smattering of short poems by the most human-seeming, approachable, and passionate of all the Roman poets. The Catullus poems I encountered in Flewett and Pantin were a revelation. They did not just spark my love of Latin poetry; they helped open up the world of poetry and human feeling for me. They showed me that being a poet might mean nothing more or less than speaking with full human feeling. It would take many years before I could see that, for me at least, being a human being, in the fullest sense, might entail being a poet.

Catullus also revealed a side of Roman culture and society entirely different from the efficiency of Caesar's military campaigns or the meticulousness of the construction of Roman roads, whose details we studied under the disciplinarian Jack "the Ripper" Anderson. These bored me as, I later found out, they also bored the profound Horatian Louis MacNeice.

Catullus was funny, charming, rude, passionate: a poet who (unlike Horace) wore his heart on his sleeve. He was rich and independent enough not to give a damn about Caesar, or about politics in general. All he cared about was love. One of the first Catullus poems we studied was his famous lament for his mistress's dead sparrow:

Join me in mourning, all you Cupids and Venuses,
and all people of finer sensibility:
mourn the death of my girlfriend's pet sparrow—
the sparrow that was her delight and playmate,
which she loved more than anything, more than
    eyesight;
for he was a sweet bird, who knew his mistress
better than a young girl knows her own mother,
and he stayed close to her, would not stir from her lap
but hopped about, hopping here, hopping there
as he cheeped his little songs for his mistress's ears
    only—
that bird who has now traveled the road of darkness,
the bourn from which they say no traveler returns.
So curses on you, wicked gloomy things, shades
of the Underworld, devourers of everything beautiful!
What a dastardly deed! Alas, poor sparrow!
You've made my girlfriend's eyes go red with weeping!

This was Catullus at his most delicately playful; I was too young to take in the subtle range of tones, from mock tragedy to a kind of rueful envy, but I loved birds and was entranced by Catullus's tender description of the relationship between Clodia and her pet sparrow.

Another poem was starker and sadder and unmistakable in its emotional force: the noble elegy for a beloved brother. The scandalous fin de siècle artist and writer Aubrey Beardsley, who may have considered Catullus a kindred spirit, and who died even younger, at twenty-six, made a moving translation:

By ways remote and distant waters sped,
Brother, to thy sad grave-side am I come,
That I may give the last gifts to the dead,
And vainly parley with thine ashes dumb:

Since she who now bestows and now denies
Has ta'en thee, hapless brother, from mine eyes
But lo! These gifts, the heirlooms of past years,
Are made sad things to grace thy coffin shell;
Take them, all drenched with a brother's tears,
And, brother, for all time, hail and farewell!"

This was a poem we were encouraged to learn by heart, in its sonorous original Latin elegiac meter, the long spondaic feet of the first hexameter verse, "Multas per gentes et multa per aequora vectus," contrasting with the lighter dactyls of the pentameter line, "advenio has miseras, frater, ad inferias."

Catullus was a spark of life, of strong human feeling, of unmistakable beauty, in a pretty somber landscape. Doing classics at Eton in those days was not expected to be fun.

I went back recently to Rudyard Kipling's story "Regulus" from *Stalky & Co.*, imagining that it encapsulated the worst and most deadly aspects of an old-school classical education. A class on a raw November morning is forced to go through the torture of construing a particularly fiendish Horace ode—the one about the heroic, and Stoic, Roman general Regulus, captured by the Carthaginians and sent back to Rome to propose the release of some Carthaginian prisoners in exchange for himself. Knowing that he will be tortured to death if he returns to Carthage, Regulus advises the Roman senate not to accept the Carthaginians' offer. Horace does not tell us how he died, back in Carthage, but the miscellanist Aulus Gellius recounts that he had his eyelids cut off and then was forced to look at the sun.

Kipling portrays the housemaster Mr. King as a martinet, but also as a deep lover of Horace, of poetry and of the power of poetry to capture an example of moral courage and style in unforgettable language. In fact King is a brilliant and passionate teacher. For him Horace is both a classic and utterly contemporary—a living, standing rebuke to journalistic shoddiness of expression,

an always relevant commentator on the moral flabbiness of democracy. It is because he is so passionate about these things
that he rebukes his class for their lazy grammatical errors and
pushes them toward translation that is not just literally accurate but true to the spirit of Horace. Linguistic accuracy is not
merely an end in itself but an essential way of learning moral
distinctions.

Later, in his autobiography, *Something of Myself*, Kipling
says more about the teacher who was the model for Mr. King:
"There must still be masters of the same sincerity, and gramo-
phone records of such good men, on the brink of profanity, strug-
gling with a Latin form, would be more helpful to education than
bushels of printed books. C- taught me to loathe Horace for two
years; to forget him for twenty, and to love him for the rest of my
days and through many sleepless nights."

Something obviously had happened between the time of
Kipling and our time. There was the deep shadow of the two
World Wars, and especially the first, in which Kipling lost his own
son. The first war especially weighed heavily on Eton: I sometimes
wandered around the school's ancient inner quadrangle, the Clois-
ters, looking at the brass plaques listing the Etonian dead in the
Great War, young men cut down in their prime. They numbered
1,157, almost as numerous as the living boys in the school. The
wars surely represented the failure of a class of people educated
to love Horace, to believe, as Auden put it, "in the absolute value
of Greek."

Classics, to most of us in the 1970s, was hardly the most exciting of subjects. It seemed moldy, dusty, dry. Why spend so much
time on dead languages? Studying Latin and Greek was laborious, involving the learning of many irregular verbs, and might
well seem pointless; hours and hours were spent slowly working
out the sense from the convoluted forms and intricate word order.

There was also an attraction. I suppose part of it was the
satisfaction of solving a puzzle. There was the sheer sonorous-

ness of the words, in the case of Latin, and the sense of quicksilver grace and intelligence that came from the ancient Greek language, and its beautiful, remote alphabet. As we learned the languages, we also were taught something about the civilizations that had given birth to them; the more accessible Roman civilization that had reached our own wet island, imprinted roads and walls on its contours, left the remains of incongruously luxurious villas, above all marked the language. And there was ancient Greece, always a kind of shining ideal, the source of perfect forms in art, the Elgin marbles and the Athenian black-figure vases with their extraordinary concentrated energy.

At least half the teachers at Eton when I arrived there in 1970 were classicists, whose duties also included teaching divinity, which meant the Old Testament. Every weekend we were faced with the daunting double exercise of Sunday Questions and Monday Questions: the first a divinity essay and the second a test on a passage of the Old Testament.

Sunday Questions and Monday Questions felt as if they had been in place for almost as long as the Ten Commandments. But it was in fact the end of an era, or the beginning of a new era. Classics, in the old dominant form, was on the way out. English (only quite recently established as a discipline), modern languages, geography, and economics were on the way in.

The study of classics had ossified. It was being carried on because that was the way it had always been. As always, there were vested interests; classics teachers did not want to lose their jobs. But the classicists were losing the battle.

I found myself in a strange position. There was too much about the old way of teaching classics that was deadly and deadening for me to be in any way a wholehearted supporter of it. But there was also something wonderful about its sheer unlikely lack of relevance, usefulness, instrumentality—words or concepts increasingly coming to dominate all areas of life. Hidden within the apparently drab, established shell of classics was the radical potential of a discipline that paid the closest possible attention to language and thought.

One of the low points was studying Livy's history of the Carthaginian wars with the headmaster, an austere specialist in Roman inscriptions who had been brought in to restore order to the school at a time when it was rocked by drug scandals.

Michael McCrum certainly cut a commanding figure in his gown and mortarboard—someone commented that he was the only man in England who could single-handedly constitute a procession—but he was a singularly uninspiring teacher. Our classes, held in a historic classroom next to Upper School, the long seventeenth-century chamber that had been the school's main classroom for centuries, consisted mainly of being tested on and translating the chunks of Livy we had been asked to prepare. That the headmaster himself had not had much time to prepare these classes was evident in the fact that the tests ended up consisting not of ten or twenty questions but of twenty-nine or thirty-three.

At no point, as far as I can remember, did he step back to give us some idea of what Livy's history might really have been about, about who Livy himself was, who the Romans were, who the Carthaginians were: about what for Livy, writing two hundred years later, was the purpose of writing this immense history. It was a missed opportunity, for Livy was telling the story of Hannibal's attack on Rome across the Alps, one of the most daring military adventures ever undertaken.

This was probably the worst example. But in general our classics teachers did not venture far beyond the grammatical. Their job seemed to end at parsing words, construing syntax, scanning meter. About the broader, deeper meaning of the works they were teaching us, which included some of the greatest literary masterpieces in the Western canon, they remained largely silent. There were exceptions, especially my classical tutor John Roberts, in whose stiflingly warm study with its piles of books and huge, blissfully comfortable red sofas we gathered for the non-academic sessions called Private Business. Roberts read aloud to us passages from Richmond Lattimore's translation of the *Odyssey*, interspersed with short stories by Maupassant; together we read plays by Shaw. I later discovered that the deceptively owlish Roberts had been a Marxist in his youth. He was encouraging us to think outside our privileged bubble. But while he might have been a secret revolutionary, he was no fan of the lazy-minded pseudoradical talk that was becoming fashionable. In response to an antiauthoritarian rant from the trendiest member of our tutorial group, he delivered one of his typically oracular sayings: "The correct attitude to the police, Hildyard, is one of ambivalence."

I was in a strange position because I did not hate classics. For one thing I was rather good at the subject and regularly came top in my year. Through a system of rewards (and punishments, though I avoided those), distinctions, commendations, prizes, we were trained and encouraged to compete as hard as any ancient Greek athlete, and I prided myself on my competitive prowess.

A noncompetitive side of learning classics was what we called construe groups: small bunches of us gathered together in someone's room in the early evening, after class and before dinner, to prepare the chunk of Virgil or Livy or Tacitus we would be tested on the next day. At least this was a collaborative activity, and I have warm memories of candlelit construe groups, preparing Book 2 of the *Aeneid*, during the blackout winter of 1972, when miners' strikes led to a state of emergency and a three-day workweek.

Horace, meanwhile, was waiting in the wings. My first encounter with him came in the sixth form, when Book 1 of the Odes was an A level set text. By this stage my relationship with classics had become more complicated. Or you could say the ambivalence had deepened.

A man I liked—a tough and intelligent New Zealander, and excellent rugby player—called John Lewis taught us Horace.

But he was too practical, too much of a Roman Stoic, to be able to open the door more than a fraction to the sensuous and Epicurean sides of Horace. His interest was more in Horace's way of accommodating himself to the Augustan regime than in his insistence on maintaining his independence. He gave little hint of the Horace who had inspired poets, free thinkers, antidogmatists throughout two millennia of Western civilization.

Still, the door did open, to let in the winter sunlight of the Soracte ode.

> Do you see the depth of snowfall,
> On Soracte standing bright? This frost
> Has stopped the rivers in their tracks;
> The trees are bowed with their white, heavy pall.
>
> In here we're warm. Keep piling logs, Hugh,
> On the blazing fire—and let's uncork
> A mellow four-year-old riserva,
> Just the Sabine vino, not a fancy cru.
>
> Give up trying to control the weather; some god
> Will calm the raging storm at sea.
> The tall flame-cypresses and the ancient ash
> Won't always shake and bend and madly nod.

Here was a Horace poem I could unreservedly like, though I could not yet grasp the logic of its swift, abrupt transitions. This was not a propaganda poem, and seemed to have very little to do with the Augustan regime, or any regime. It was suffused with light—crisp Mediterranean winter sunlight—and with warmth, the physical warmth of the log fire, the warming power of wine, friendship, and camaraderie.

Years later I read how that poem by Horace had forged an unlikely friendship. The scene was the mountains of Crete, the time the spring of 1944, two months before the D-day landings. A dashing group of young British and Cretan Special Operations commandos led by Major Paddy Leigh Fermor had kidnapped the German military governor of Crete, Major General Heinrich Kreipe, in the Cretan capital, Heraklion. They had then brought him by shepherds' pathways up the massif of Mount Ida, aiming for the south coast, where a boat would take them to Egypt.

Looking out at the white-topped mountains, maybe wondering how he could escape, calculating the risks, the general suddenly had another thought, or a recollection. He began to recite the first line, "Vides ut alta stet nive candidum Soracte." His British captor continued the stanza, and the one after, in which the poet brings the focus from the frozen winter landscape to a warm room with a log fire and wine generously poured, and the one after that, to the magical end of the poem, in which winter has been replaced by heady summer, the meeting of young lovers in the hidden corners of the warm squares of Rome. "It was very strange," recalls Leigh Fermor; "we had both drunk at the same fountains long before; and things were different between us for the rest of our time together."

This was a Roman poem, but had nothing to do with the prosaic Roman world of legions and drainage ditches. Caesar's cold-eyed "veni, vidi, vici" (I came, I saw, I conquered) had been replaced by Horace's warm "vixi" (I have lived).

Or was it a Roman poem? You could say it was an Italian poem, but its mysterious power and beauty had other roots. Like so many other Roman artworks, it was simultaneously Italian and Greek. The music for a start was Greek, which quite possibly had been Horace's first language. So maybe to appreciate Horace more fully it was necessary to visit Greece. Hadn't Horace counseled, in the *Ars Poetica*, the constant perusing of Greek models?

Signing up for a school classics trip to Greece at age seventeen was one of the best and most liberating things I did at Eton.

The master in charge, Nigel Jaques, the most gently civilized of Eton classicists, applied a slack rein; suddenly we felt the dead hand of discipline and the fear of contravening rules magically lifted. Jaques trusted us not to get into too much trouble. One evening, after a taverna supper on the Plaka, a boy from the year below me called Paul Highett and I consumed so much retsina, accompanied by street-stall kebabs, that for several years afterward the faintest whiff of a kebab made me feel sick.

On our first morning in Athens, a day of pristine April sunshine, I climbed up to the Acropolis, walking past the exquisite octagonal Tower of the Winds in the Roman agora built when Horace was a boy. I had pored over photographs in books of the great buildings erected under Pericles, the gateway of the Propylaea, the little temple of Nike, the Erechtheion with its much-copied caryatids, the Parthenon itself. Nothing had prepared me for their splendor in the bright, white materiality of their Pentelic marble, especially the magnificence of the Parthenon as the sun caught the hewn stone. Jaques had taught us something about the sophistication of the building, the way slight curves and irregularities (the bulging, or entasis, of the columns) played against the apparent simplicity and monotony of the structure. Now I could see how grandeur and lightness could coexist. In those days there were no barriers, gates, or guards, and I wandered happily over the site for more than an hour, taking photographs, peering down from the table-topped rock to the theaters cut into its sides, and, farther away, to the views all around, south to the port of Piraeus and the islands of the Saronic Gulf, north, east, and west to the mountains of Hymettus, Penteli, and Parnitha. You could fall in love simply with the names.

What took my breath away repeatedly on that trip was the beauty of the Greek architectural sites, not the landscape on its own, stunning as it was, not the temples, theaters, palaces abstracted from the landscape, but the way they grew out of it and reflected its beauty back. After Athens, we crossed into the Peloponnese en route for Mycenae, Tiryns, and the superb fourth-century B.C. theater of Epidaurus.

I stood on the round acting area of the stone theater with its radiating rows of marble benches, enough to seat fifteen thousand, and recited some lines by Euripides, to test the famous acoustics. I was especially attracted to a theater, because of the enthusiasm for theater that had been nurtured at Eton, where I had acted in plays on our splendid modern thrust stage, where perhaps I had managed to feel fully myself only in the guise of another; maybe also I felt that the site at Epidaurus, a tree-rich oasis nestling in the dry hills of the Peloponnese, really was a sanctuary, a healing place, dedicated to the healing god Asklepios. Certainly I needed such a place.

After Epidaurus came Sparta, a nondescript modern town with a great ancient name; and then over the beetling Taygetus Mountains to Pylos, Nestor's town, where we played soccer with local lads. Not far from Pylos, but approachable only with difficulty along a slow high mountain road, was one of the greatest and most remote sites in Greece: the fifth-century B.C. temple of Apollo at Bassae, architecturally revolutionary with its use of all three orders of columns, Doric, Ionic, and Corinthian, standing gray and indomitable on a high ridge.

We traveled around in a minibus driven by Nikos, who at the end of the trip would invite us to drinks with his wife and family in a flat in Athens. The camaraderie of the bus rides, and the evening meals at tavernas, washed down with rough Peloponnesian retsina served from the barrel, maybe not so different from the country wine of classical times, were just as important as the serious educational business of the sites. But these were genuinely thrilling: I thought Delphi was the most spectacularly beautiful place I had ever seen, deserving its title of omphalos, or belly button of the earth; the central, radiating point of Greek civilization; and we ran relay races in the stadium.

We also set out on a ferry to visit that other Greek center, the treeless bare island of Delos, covered in marble remains. Blue sky, blue Aegean, green grass already browning and the white columns still standing. One thing Nigel Jaques had not counted on was the fact that our choice of hotel on the island of Mykonos was a popular one with the burgeoning Mykonos gay scene.

Without knowing it I had made one connection with Horace; he too had traveled to Greece, at a similar age, and had his life transformed. His deepening study of Greek poetry and philosophy would mark his poetry, which is unthinkable without them. In Greece he also would be caught up in a wave of political enthusiasm and experience his short-lived but high-flying military career in the army of Brutus.

A more direct connection with Horace came right at the end of my time at Eton, when finally free of examinations I came to write an essay grandly entitled "Wine and Western Civilization" for the Essay Society, a somewhat pompous and self-important body of senior boys that met monthly in the headmaster's drawing room. But I enjoyed writing the essay, and found not only that my guiding thread was Horace but that I had discovered a new and more satisfactory way of approaching and understanding him. That essay, now that I look back on it, seems like the start of something really important—or of various things. For a start it was a truly wide-ranging essay, a form I found congenial. It approached both wine and Western civilization from unexpected angles that would prove fruitful. And as for the Horace connection, I had no idea how far that would take me.

I am still not sure whether my Eton education opened more doors than it closed. It turned out that I would not be interested in the openings to worldly wealth and influence for which it was most obviously designed. But there was a tradition of Etonian men of letters, which had included the great radical atheist and Hellenist poet Percy Bysshe Shelley, the satirist Aldous Huxley, and the socialist essayist and novelist George Orwell. My old-fashioned classical education had, in the end, prepared me well for that, even if there were times when I, like Kipling, loathed not just Horace, but the whole dry and dusty apparatus of classical learning presented merely as grammar and facts.

Doors open and close not just outward but inward. A public school education is commonly supposed to produce confident young men and women, equipped with charm and social grace. I didn't feel confident in the least when I left Eton; socially maladroit and painfully aware of how narrow was my knowledge of the Other, which included, most important, girls, and people from different races and backgrounds. Sexually, emotionally, I was all at sea. But perhaps I can't blame the school for that.

Five

The Scholars

Cambridge University was always going to have difficulty living up to the high hopes I had for it while wandering around Paris, the North and South Atlantic, and South America in my gap year (I spent time as an au pair, worked my passage to Rio in a banana boat, ended up in a Peruvian jail). Somehow all aspects of being, intense intellectual inquiry, passionate love, and partying were going to come together in a grand synthesis. I had chosen my college, Trinity, purely on aesthetic grounds: the irregular Great Court with its fountain was surely the most beautiful place in England.

But when I arrived at Trinity I discovered that my bedsit was located nowhere near Great Court but above commercial premises on Sidney Street, approached from the gloomy neo-Gothic entrance of Whewell's Court via an obscure rat run of passages and stairways over roofs, in what seemed quite another part of town.

This disappointment was accompanied by others. Starting the classics course, I found that the approach to literature and poetry in particular was philological, not literary critical. Scholars such as my director of studies, Roger Dawe, cultivated an extreme dryness that derived from A. E. Housman (another Trinity don) in his guise as Cambridge Professor of Latin rather than as poet. All trace of emotion had to be expunged in the analysis of literary texts, because the object was not anything as fatuously subjective as amateurish appreciation, but rather the surgically precise restoration of the damaged or disputed text.

In other words, everything I had learned from my brilliant English teachers at school, about the possibility of a personal, emotive approach to literary criticism, opening onto wide vistas of the world, either had to be unlearned or put aside. In his poem "The Scholars," W. B. Yeats rages at the stale old academic pedants who have become the gatekeepers of the Latin love poets. "Bald heads, forgetful of your sins," he rants, summoning up a picture of a shuffling procession in dandruff-encrusted corduroy jackets and stained trousers. These men—this is before the days of women classicists—are experts at editing and annotating lines but have completely forgotten what it might have been like to be Catullus, say, or Propertius, or Horace.

They are dull, conventional, inauthentic; if the real Catullus, a passionate, lovelorn poet, not unlike the young Yeats in the throes of his unrequited love for Maud Gonne, suddenly appeared among them, they would not have the first idea what to say to him.

Yeats had put his finger on it: here were pedants whose knowledge of the letter of the text seemed entirely unaccompanied by any profound understanding of what might have brought the text into being.

I spent a couple of weeks pacing the Backs, coming to what seemed a momentous decision. I was going to give up classics, the subject in which I had excelled and won a scholarship, and change to English, the only faculty that welcomed emotion.

What I wanted to say to Roger Dawe, but couldn't at the time, was something like this: you think you are salvaging the classics with your textual criticism, by correcting the minutest corruptions (a word beloved by textual critics), but surely what the classics need is something entirely different. What does a minor corruption matter when the whole beautiful intricate vessel of classical literature, like the many-masted man-of-war in Turner's painting *The Fighting Temeraire*, is being towed away to oblivion?

What is needed more urgently is a discussion and articulation of why classical literature, and classical poetry in particular, matters. Surely it matters because it still speaks to us, still moves us. I knew that because of Catullus, because a few of his poems had spoken to me and moved me at school. I knew that because of Horace, some of whose poems I found impenetrable, while others I was beginning to love.

And here at Cambridge I was beginning to read the Greek lyric poets who had inspired and acted as models for Horace, or the pitiful fragments of some of the greatest literature ever written, still communicating the intensest personal emotion, the passion or obsession or infatuation Sappho felt for some girl or other on the island of Lesbos, the magnificent hatred of Archilochus.

This was emotion that had stood the test of time and felt miraculously as fresh as if it were being felt right now (because it had been poured into the right, lasting vessels); it was something these human beings had felt and spoken two and a half thousand years ago to prove they were human and to bear witness to the human.

How could you approach this poetry as if it had nothing to do with emotion (heaven forbid that you yourself should show any emotion)? Perhaps these perverse classicists were devotees of the rites of Attis as described in Catullus's strangest poem: self-castrators.

In fact my director of studies' hero, A. E. Housman, had on at least one occasion let slip his mask of impassivity. The time was May 1914, a time that hindsight makes especially poignant, the last spring "with blossom hung along the bough" before the carnage of the First World War, which Housman had somehow prophesied in the lyrics of *A Shropshire Lad*, published in 1895. The place was a lecture hall in the classics faculty at Cambridge University. Housman had been analyzing a poem by Horace—the

seventh ode from Book 4, the poem about spring and the fleet-
ingness of human life that begins "the snows have fled"—in a
virtuoso but emotionless display of scholarship.

Suddenly he spoke to the class in a different, humbler tone:
"I should like to spend the last few minutes considering this ode
simply as poetry." He proceeded to read it aloud, in a voice laden
with emotion, first in Latin, then in his own English translation.
By the end students noticed that the famously dry professor's
eyes were filling with tears. "That I regard as the most beautiful
poem in ancient literature," he managed to blurt out, before turning around and walking hurriedly from the room.

A whole strangulated emotional economy is encapsulated in
that story. It was not that Housman did not understand the profound emotional content of poetry, and Horace's exquisite ode;
he understood and felt it all too keenly. But his own emotional
economy was subject to strict, self-imposed constraints. A poet
of a later generation, W. H. Auden, also homosexual, attempted to
psychoanalyze Housman's retreat from unbearable or unacceptable emotion—his love of rough trade—into a dry scholarship
that was a form of self-hate, into which he could at least channel
the emotions of cold anger and contempt. Housman, in what you
could see as an act of self-punishment, chose to devote many
years to an edition not of Horace or Propertius, the poets he really loved, but of Manilius, a minor Roman versifier whose long
didactic poem on astrology must rank as one of the most obscure
in the entire annals of poetry.

It was time, finally, for me to break with all that. I did not
regret my decision to read English; it felt inevitable, connected
to who I was as a person. Sure enough, in the English faculty I
would discover more of my tribe: that is, would-be writers, would-
be journalists, as well as would-be theater and film directors, one
or two actors.

Reading English did not mean breaking entirely with classics. In fact it led to a new and more liberating relationship with

Latin and Greek literature. Studying the literature of one foreign language was a requirement for Part I of the English Tripos. I found myself studying Latin literature with a most unusual, then itinerant, classicist called Mick Comber. Mick wore a leather jacket, was a Marxist film critic, and drove an Alfa Romeo. In all those respects he was quite different from any of my previous classics teachers. I liked the informality of our classes, which sometimes happened outdoors, in Trinity Fellows' Garden, and put the texts under discussion—Virgil's Eclogues—into new and unfamiliar frames. I liked being, and being taught by, an unofficial classicist, not an official one (though eventually Mick would become a thoroughly official classicist, a don at Christ Church Oxford). I had the company of my friend George Myerson, the beginnings of a dialogue about Roman poetry, and many other matters without which this book never would have been written.

Later I would accept Mick's offer of extracurricular classes in Greek, which consisted of reading Euripides's *Bacchae*, a play that entranced Horace, in the original. I had the feeling that Mick's greatest love was film, especially the cinema of the Russian Revolution. He saw parallels between Eisenstein's use of montage and the equally dislocating cutting of narrative perspectives in Tacitus's *Histories* and in Horace's Odes. It was fascinating stuff but I found that his interest in classical literature veered between the extremely technical—he had a special interest in the work of Tycho von Wilamowitz-Moellendorff, a classicist of great promise killed in the First World War and the son of the greatest of all German classical philologists, Ulrich von Wilamowitz-Moellendorff—and the ideological, the way Greek drama prefigured Marxian dialectics.

Something was still missing from this approach, though I was most grateful to Mick for keeping my Latin and Greek going, in some form, with enthusiasm and friendliness. What was missing was, simply put, a subjective, emotionally engaged kind of literary criticism applied to classical texts. Or you could say a deeply personal approach to classical poetry, the feeling, shared by so many poets and others down the ages—from Petrarch to Jonson, Voltaire, Leopardi, and Nietzsche—that Horace, or Catullus, or Sappho, was not a "text" to be approached with the objectivity of the scholar, but a friend, a source of solace and wisdom. Mick, for all his formidable intellectual strengths, was still suspicious of that.

In fact the subjective approach I favored was going out of fashion even in the English faculty, which I found to be convulsed by bitter academic acrimony. This came to a head with the refusal of tenure to the structuralist literary critic and lecturer Colin MacCabe in 1981, a cause célèbre in which the two biggest beasts of Cambridge English, the traditionalist Christopher Ricks and the more theoretically minded Frank Kermode, were bitterly opposed.

What all this signified was the approach, or invasion, of the good ship theory, crossing the Channel rather belatedly, laden with the heady ideas that had brought students onto the streets, and toppled a government, in Paris in May 1968. Theory was a mixture of Nietzschean relativism, Freudian and Lacanian psychoanalysis, Debordian Situationism, but above all the combination of Saussurian linguistics and Lévi-Straussian structural anthropology.

How could all this fail to be exciting and stimulating? How could any young person of mettle want to reject all this in favor of the old, gentleman's club version of literary criticism? Horribile dictu, dear reader, I did. Some parts of "theory" I would later find both fascinating and liberating, bits of psychoanalysis in particular. But the version of theory that was beginning to influence literary studies, the structuralist poetics promoted by Jonathan Culler and others, seemed in an odd way to share some of the least attractive aspects of the old dry textual criticism. Perhaps it also had some of the same origins and motivations— the desire to move from a wishy-washy, unstable subjectivism to firmer, quasi-scientific ground. Lévi-Strauss had found certain rules, relating to kinship, cooking, shame, that applied across cultures; Saussure had argued that languages were essentially systems of differentiation, whose individual features lacked intrinsic meaning. In his famous 1967 essay Roland Barthes proposed "the death of the author." All this seemed to leave literature as a sort of machine for generating meanings, in which larger cultural and structural elements were far more important than individual quirks of style.

Theory was in part an exercise of power, shifting emphasis from self-indulgent authors, marinated in outdated sentiment, to cold clinical theoreticians, standing in some way outside their own cultures in order, mercilessly, to expose their contradictions. It reminded me of the conversation in David Lean's film version of Pasternak's *Dr. Zhivago* (I had read the novel with passionate enthusiasm at age sixteen) between two of Lara's lovers—Zhivago himself, the divided but deeply human doctor and poet, and Strelnikov, the terrifying cold ideologue, willing to sacrifice anything and anyone to the greater good. "Feelings, insights, affections . . . it's all suddenly trivial now," says Strelnikov. "You don't agree; you're wrong. The personal life is dead in Russia. History has killed it . . . the private life is dead—for a man with any manhood."

I could not accept the idea of the death of the author, not just because I felt sustained by relationships with authors, but because it also would imply my own death, as a would-be author. Where would the death of the author leave the poet, especially the lyric poet, speaking with the voice of interiority and subjectivity?

One afternoon after watching a film at the Arts Cinema, a wonderful womblike place in a passageway near the market, where I always felt happy—I began to write a short story about the death of the Italian painter Caravaggio. I carried on late into the night and experienced a kind of road-to-Damascus conversion. I had to be a writer, a creative writer (whatever that overused word might mean), there was no other way; nothing would ever give me so much intense pleasure and satisfaction. The short story was eventually published in the *Trinity Review*, together with a brilliant tale about a man who discovered God, a discovery that a trivial media-obsessed society entirely failed to grasp, by George Myerson. It would be followed by a few others, which I sent to the novelist John Fowles and about which he made some encouraging comments. But how all this linked to the academic study of English, or to Horace, was something of a mystery.

Otherwise time at Cambridge passed with the intensity that you take for granted at that age. There were the beginnings of friendships that would last, others that would not; there were agonizing, usually unrequited yearnings; unwise confidences made to the wrong people. There were attempts at acting—which I was not good at—and directing, for which I had a little more talent. There was student journalism and tennis and wine tasting and innumerable parties. But there was also deep and incommunicable unhappiness, probably mostly of a fairly simple and sexual nature.

The third year of the degree course, compressed into just three eight-week terms of epic intensity, is meant to be the time when you think seriously about what you will do next, in the real world. The real world, as defined by such professions and institutions as the Civil Service, the Bar, even the Hong Kong Police Force, had little attraction for me. I had decided I wanted to be a writer but had no idea how to achieve this goal. One thing I was pretty sure I could do was defer the decision: embark on a PhD, funded by a government studentship, while continuing with my creative writing.

My plan for the PhD was to research twentieth-century translations of Greek tragedy, in particular those by Yeats and Ezra Pound. And behind that plan was another, more shadowy one: to look at the continuing relevance, or indeed the resurgence, of Greek tragedy and especially the plays of Sophocles in the twentieth century: in the work of Freud, whose most important single idea came in the form of a Greek myth dramatized by Sophocles; in Richard Strauss's opera *Elektra*; in the cinema of Pasolini and others; in the radical new revisionings of Greek tragedy by the Royal Shakespeare Company and other groups that were being staged in Britain in the late 1970s.

Such a plan, I soon realized, was far too vague, ambitious, and far-reaching to make an acceptable PhD topic. My work started with Ezra Pound and Sophocles. Pound, at a time when he was in extremis, had made a version of Sophocles's *Women of Trachis*, movingly connecting his own madness with the tortured ravings of Heracles in the terrible straitjacket of the shirt of Nessus.

More generally, Pound had been inspired with a vision of the continuing relevance, the modernity, of classical texts, under his banner of "Make it new." For Pound classics had never been an establishment discipline; the classical texts, or at least fragments of them, were living, vital parts of world literature, as alive and vital as the classical Chinese poems he had come across in the versions of Ernest Fenellosa and turned into the startlingly fresh lyrics of *Cathay*, or the aubades of the Provençal troubadours. Early in his life Pound had preferred Propertius to Horace; in a famous 1930 essay he had attacked Horace for being "neither simple nor passionate . . . bald-headed, pot-bellied, underbred, sycophantic, less poetic than any other great master of literature"; later still, after his own life's shipwreck on the rocks of overfervent belief in fascism, he had come back to the Odes and translated three of them, including "Aere perennius" and "Carpe diem," with an inspired stony roughness.

My plan turned out to be flawed. Stuck in a rather remote, suburban part of Cambridge, I immersed myself in the Greek texts of Sophocles's tragedies. It was a solitary business, and it led, perhaps unsurprisingly, to melancholy. This was in part purely personal, but it was also connected to a feeling that the poetic beauty and dramatic power of Sophocles's texts were essentially incommunicable, or untranslatable. The beauty and power, as with Shakespeare, resided in the language itself. I had the feeling of these great shining works receding, inevitably, as the languages ceased to be studied.

For a while I found some traction in applying the techniques of literary criticism I had learned studying English—that is to say a kind of close reading that concentrated on the emotional meanings of poetic language—to Sophocles. It seemed to work; I gave a seminar on the great, deceptive messenger speech in *Electra* to a group of classicists, who found my approach novel; my charming and friendly supervisor, Patricia Easterling, was impressed, and when we met, rather infrequently, she assured me I was doing fine.

Unfortunately I could not convince myself of this. After a year I could take no more. It wasn't just that I could no longer motivate myself to read Sophocles, and do my research into Ezra Pound's translation of *Women of Trachis*, but that I felt I had come to the end of a blind alley.

This whole educational avenue that I had followed, more or less without question, being a scholar at Eton and Cambridge, because I seemed to be good at it, had ended in unnavigable darkness. It was like one of those French roads marked "sans issu." I hadn't yet come to the realization that the way back to the classics would involve my own rebirth as a writer.

Six

"I Set Out Alone"

Horace, nearly always the most economical of writers, is especially economical when it comes to writing about his greatest adventure. But the very little he reveals about his time in Athens—the place privileged young Romans went for their equivalent of a university education—makes it clear that this was a very special period in his life.

He speaks about that time in one of the last of all his poems, the letter to Florus in Book 2 of the Epistles:

> Rome was where I had the luck to grow up; to learn
> My Homer, how Achilles's anger hurt the Greeks.
> Athens, best of cities, gave me art and skill,
> Encouraged me to know the crooked from the straight,
> To search for truth in the sacred wood of the Academy.
> But hard times ripped me from that lovely place;
> Civil war's tsunami flung me, unfit for war,
> Into unequal combat with great Caesar's power.

I don't think you can miss the powerful feeling there, of love and regret. And to speak so warmly of Athens, the center of Greek culture, and especially Greek philosophy, is to make quite a strong statement. In general Romans in Horace's time had to be ambivalent about Greece. The days when the elder Cato could lead an anti-Hellenic movement were long gone. Greek culture had permeated Rome. Greek philosophy, poetry, art, architecture were the models. As Horace says in his letter to Augustus, "Captive Greece captured its savage victor, and instilled the arts into rustic Rome."

But elsewhere in that same letter (addressed to the head of state, and reinstaller of antique Roman virtues) Horace himself has to be ambivalent, or hypocritical. Yes, Greece was great for art and philosophy, but the Greeks were a decadent lot. "Once she'd finished her wars, Greece became silly; slipped into bad habits in the easy times. She fell in love now with athletes, now with horses; her passion was for sculptors and carvers; she fixed her mind and soul on painted panels; she was besotted with flautists and tragic actors; like a baby girl playing with her nurse, she flung away the toys she begged for." (Far-off pre-echoes here of the strange contempt for all things French that swept America at the time of the Iraq invasion in 2003, the talk of surrender monkeys and freedom fries; or, further down the line, of the contempt toward financially stricken Greece shown by those who should have known better.)

All this in contrast, of course, to the rugged, hardworking, and practical Romans, up at dawn, doing business, passing on property, and avoiding riotous excess. In fact Horace's tongue is firmly in his cheek here, because he knows, and he knows the princeps knows, that he is not a Roman of that stamp, but a Hellenized one addicted to writing verses. And in fact that addiction or passion is not so vicious after all, because poets are not grasping or cheating types. The poet may be a poor soldier and slow at working in the fields, but he does the state some service. He "gives form to the child's tender stammering mouth . . . and molds the heart with friendly rules." Teaching children to speak and instilling a moral philosophy: not such a small service after all.

All that came, in a way, from Greece. Horace's love of Greece, his sadness at being ripped away from the place that taught him how to think and how to write, must have been profound. How he actually spent his days in Athens, other than by studying philosophy and poetry, we can only guess, or get at indirectly. The best documented case of a wealthy young Roman and contemporary of Horace studying in Athens is that of Cicero's son Marcus, the boy in whom the great orator had so much hope, who turned out to be such a disappointment.

Marcus, from Cicero's letters in which he is mentioned at length, sounds in some ways a more normal kind of young man than Horace. He has good intentions, he wants to study, but he is all too often distracted by the fleshpots, drinking, dissolution of all kinds. He undoubtedly had a good deal more money than young Horace, and less intellectual ability. Marcus's letters to his father are full of promises to reform. His father's letters are rueful, indulgent, always willing to give the boy another chance.

But in one respect Marcus may have been better equipped than Horace. Marcus and Horace were studying in Athens at a momentous time. They must have arrived there around 44 B.C., the time of Caesar's murder. A couple of years later Brutus the tyrant killer swept into town. At first, according to Plutarch's *Life*, Brutus appeared to be "engaged in philosophical pursuits" and to "have laid aside all thought of public business." But that was a front. He was "secretly making preparation for war," that is to say a war against the second triumvirate, led by Mark Antony and Octavian (later to become Augustus), the avengers of Caesar's murder. Soon Brutus had "won over and kept at his disposal all the young Romans that were then studying at Athens." These included Marcus and Horace, both in their early twenties. Brutus seems to have had a high regard for Marcus: "He could not choose but admire a young man of so great a spirit and such a hater of tyranny." The only question for Brutus, according to Plutarch, was this one: "whether they should live or die free men."

This was also the question that preoccupied Horace, in ways perhaps more varied than Brutus could have imagined, throughout his life. I think we can guess that Horace was a hater of tyranny too.

Young Horace went to serve on Brutus's staff as a "military tribune." According to Peter Levi in his *Horace: A Life*, such "tribunes could be anything from aristocratic youths getting experience to agreeable companions chosen for their conversational or literary talents." Marcus probably fell into the first category, Horace into the second.

Agreeable companion, conversationalist, poet-to-be he may have been, but that did not stop Horace from being a soldier. He was fighting in the Roman world's equivalent of the Spanish Civil War, the poets' and idealists' war. But this war involved large-scale plunder. Both Brutus and Cassius, leaving Athens and heading first in different directions, went around the provinces of the eastern empire, extorting soldiers and money from the local rulers. When they resisted, whole cities were put to the sword and the flame. Horace, who must have been there, does not tell us what he thought.

The campaign came to a head in one great and dreadful battle (actually two battles), one of the worst disasters ever to befall Rome in terms of numbers of promising young Romans killed, the battle of Philippi in October–November 42 B.C.

In the first part of the engagement Cassius's army, encamped by marshes, was defeated by Mark Antony's forces. To the north, Brutus's troops attacked and overran Octavian's camp. Octavian himself, according to Livy, went and "hid in some marshes." But now confusion took its toll. Cassius heard a false report that Brutus had been defeated and committed suicide. All the same the first battle had been a kind of draw. Twenty days later the forces of Brutus and what was left of Cassius's army faced Antony and Octavian and were soundly defeated. Brutus, in great nobility of spirit, fell on his sword.

Horace tells us none of this. But neither does he ever try to deny that he fought at Philippi, and fought on the losing side. As Fraenkel said, "He might have passed over in silence the days of Philippi and all they implied for him. In fact, however, he did the very opposite." He maintained warm friendships with comrades-in-arms such as Messalla Corvinus and Pompeius Varus.

All that Horace says about what happened to him at Philippi is that he left his shield ignominiously behind ("parmula non bene relicta") on the battlefield, and that Mercury helped him escape in a cloud. The shield bit has sounded quite real and convincing to some people, the cloud bit obviously poetic license. But the image of the shield left on the battlefield appears in at least one of Horace's Greek models, Archilochus, and possibly others, so that may not be literally true either.

Something Horace does not say anywhere is that the battle was a noble affair. It sounds more like the description of Borodino in *War and Peace*, or Matthew Arnold's "ignorant armies" clashing "by night" in "Dover Beach." The mention of Mercury, his patron god, helping him escape in a cloud is another way of saying he was lucky, as so many were not. What Horace thought about that internecine slaughter he makes clear in one of the most savage poems he ever wrote, Epode 7.

"Can't you see you're rushing headlong into ruin?
Why do your right hands grasp once-sheathed swords?
Do you think too little Roman blood's been spilled
On far-flung fields and in the ocean deeps?
. . . Is it just blind madness, or some stronger power,
Or is it guilt which drives us on?"

No sign of "dulce et decorum" there; these are lines that Wilfred Owen himself might have written—the later Wilfred Owen, that is, bitterly skewering Horace's old lie from the trenches, not the naive early Owen who wrote "The Ballad of Peace and War":

O meet it is and passing sweet
To live in peace with others
But sweeter still and far more meet
To die in war for brothers.

So what price "dulce et decorum est pro patria mori"—did Horace really mean it? Or perhaps the better question is how exactly did Horace mean it?

No one ever quotes the lines that come after "dulce et decorum." The meaning of the whole stanza is this: "Yes, it is sweet and fitting to die for your country. But death catches up in the end with the man who runs away; death does not spare the quaking knees of those who do not want to fight." The universal condition of mankind, condemned to inevitable death, suddenly comes to seem just as important as dying for your country as a brave soldier.

The truth is that there is more than one way of dying bravely. The ode turns out to be not really about the soldier at all, but about the quality Horace calls "virtus." This quality, call it courage, can belong to any principled person, a civilian who stands up to the vengeful or envious crowd, even a poet who spurns easy popularity, just as much as to a soldier.

Horace had been prepared to lay down his life for a cause, for a nobler idea of Rome that included the ability to live in freedom. But his side had lost; he had escaped, somehow, in the confusion, not nobly but not ignobly either. He had escaped with his death-limited life.

In retrospect it seems to me that my true university education did not take place in Cambridge. Like Horace I needed to be immersed in another culture, another country, another language. Thoroughly fed up with aspects of my life and my class in England, I decided to decamp to Spain. I arrived in Barcelona one morning in September 1983, bleary-eyed after a twenty-four-hour bus journey, lugging an enormous suitcase, which contained, among other things, an Adler portable typewriter. I had precisely one contact; that would prove to be enough.

My time in Barcelona seems like an exercise in minimalism, in the Horatian art of living with less, though I would not have put it that way then. All my possessions, for a start, were reduced to what I could carry in that big suitcase. In terms of weight, that meant mainly books, as well as the Adler. Books would never mean more to me than they did then, but I found I could live with fewer—and there was always the British Council library, and the whole of Spanish literature to be explored as I became more fluent in reading the language.

Possessions are one thing, but friends are another—the last thing human beings can do without, according to Aristotle, with whom Horace certainly would have agreed. My one contact in Barcelona, a Canadian called Chris Robinson, proved remarkably fertile and sustaining. Through him, very quickly, I found somewhere to live—quite minimal, a room in a shared flat right underneath Gaudí's exuberant church of the Sagrada Família, in a modern and undistinguished but perfectly friendly part of town, and amazingly cheap, the equivalent of seven pounds a week in rent. There were sometimes five people sharing one bathroom and one basic kitchen, with a stone sink and no kettle; some of the rooms had no windows, but I was happier there, in my cell-like room looking out onto the tiny patio with its lemon tree and, suspended above, the pineapple pinnacles of the Sagrada Família, than I have been in much grander accommodation.

I became friends with Chris, who was teaching English, his Spanish girlfriend, Mari, Chris's quiet, observant brother Garth, and a Californian guitarist named Ricky Araiza. Ricky would become my guide to the bars and boîtes of Barcelona where he played jazz and bluegrass. There was an immediate and unlikely chemistry between us, the uptight old Etonian scholar and the loose Californian musician, which could only partly be explained by Ricky's love of all things English. The irony was that I was in full flight from all those things.

These four would remain my rock, a loyal band of muske- teers who never let me down. I discovered something very dif- ferent from the frenetic, competitive socializing of Cambridge: that one could live very well and happily with three or four good friends.

Then of course there was the city, not then the trendy, sleek Euro-place it has become, but a pungent and fascinating blend of styles of architecture, of layers of history, of political intensity, of different languages and cultures, in particular the subtle and sometimes jarring play of Catalan against Castellano, of physical enjoyments, of intellectual and artistic excitement, of well-padded bourgeois wealth and comfort set against Dickensian poverty, and beyond that something ineffable and unique: the spirit of Barcelona, which had emerged time and again over history, tak- ing forms such as the sober gray-stone magnificence of the Gothic quarter, the utopian idealism of the Eixample, the city extension beyond the walls planned as a garden suburb, the vi- sionary Catholic-organicist genius of Gaudí, the artistic ferment of the early twentieth century around Els Quatre Gats, the un- repeatable moment of July 1936 when anarchy in its noblest form briefly flowered in the city.

Chris and Mari lived somewhere much more romantic than my functional quarters, in a dark but aristocratic flat in the car- rer Brosolí, in part of the medieval city not far from the sailors' church of Santa María del Mar. The houses were built of great stone blocks; the streets were so narrow that you could almost lean out of the window and touch the other side (you could cer- tainly hang washing across); but the lack of light seemed poetic, not gloomy. In the carrer de l'Argenteria just outside there was one of Barcelona's smartest restaurants, which we never set foot in, and a friendly family-run bar (Domingo, where we often went for Sunday tapas). All around were anarchist or surrealist bars with names like Suceso.

Suceso means "happening," not "success"; an emphasis on success would come much later; for the time being, young people in Barcelona were more into happening, in the great catching-up from forty years of gloomy Catholic-Fascist dictatorship. These bars stayed open till three or four; if you asked for a whiskey or anís, you would just be given the bottle. The invitation was to pour to your heart's content.

One of the great things about being in Barcelona was that I was always learning. Every time I visited a café or bar or bakery, let alone a church or museum, every time I picked up *El País*, the excellent Spanish newspaper that was one of the first and best fruits of the transition to democracy (I especially liked the opinion pieces by dissident philosophers such as José Luis Aranguren), I would be improving my Spanish, at the same time as having it adulterated with Catalan, which I never learned to speak properly. Every step I took in the city involved a kind of historical and personal deepening and broadening. Perhaps Horace felt that way about Athens.

It was not just about learning facts but about learning ways to be. Spaniards, and here I include Catalans in that category, seemed to be at home in their bodies, and on the streets, in a way that the English, or the English I knew, could only dream of.

Several times that autumn, in the blessed mildness and golden light of Catalonian October, I took the train down the coast to the seaside town of Sitges. I would eat fish near the seafront, swim in the still-warm Med, and take a train back in the late afternoon.

On one of those train journeys, hugging the rocky coast, wearing summer clothes, with all the windows open, in one of those breaks between compartments, with a few other young backpackers, like the last swallows of a season, I remember feeling that at last I was living my relative youth (even if a little bit older at twenty-five than the backpackers). I was late, too late for conventional summer, too late for my own conventional university time, but I had been given another chance, and this time I was living in my own day, the Horatian day of carpe diem.

About a month later, on the Saturday of the All Saints' holiday, I was on the same train heading farther south with a classmate from my university course. Saskia was a tall, blonde Dutch girl who was frank and friendly in the no-nonsense Dutch way; she, unlike me, had Catalan friends, and invited me to go camping with them near the delta of the Ebro.

I am not a good camper, and I can still remember pitching the huge tent (it must have slept fifteen) with Saskia and the others in a howling gale and the first rain of the autumn, but I am glad I did not miss that trip.

Before nightfall, near the fishing village of L'Ametlla de Mar, we walked along the shore and climbed up to a cave where we could sit and eat hunks of *fuet* (Catalan salami) and bread smeared with tomato and garlic cut with a clasp knife and look out toward the lights of Amposta and the emptiness of the open sea.

I had never been with a bunch of young Catalans before.

They seemed gentle, artistic, musical. Someone had a guitar and sang. They were outdoor people, into hiking and being close to nature, not self-conscious about nudity. They were egalitarian and strictly nonsexist, not at all macho, opposed to bullfighting; more like Swedes or Dutch or Germans than Spaniards. I quickly realized that when a group of Catalans gathered together they would be reluctant to speak Castilian.

This meant I could only understand dribs and drabs of conversation, and, on Sunday morning, feeling somewhat isolated, I was thinking of heading back. Saskia told me there were others joining the party, including a girl who spoke very good English, "so it might be very interesting."

I don't remember exactly when the others arrived, but that evening we were all sitting in the big tent in the dark listening to the Brazilian singer Vinicius de Moraes. I found myself sitting toe-to-toe with the petite, self-possessed, gray-eyed, blonde Anna, and thought I felt the pressure of her feet against mine. Perhaps I did, but, as I realized later, it would not have meant the same to her as to me.

She had greeted me with the words "Hullo Harry," spoken with such perfect intonation that I thought it must be almost a game for her, to speak English so well. We immediately had things to talk about: English Romantic poetry, which we both loved, and German idealist philosophy, which she had studied and I had not. When she remarked "Kant is certainly an important moment," I was thoroughly impressed, perhaps even more than I should have been.

Having Anna around, as my friend (she had come with a darkly good-looking boyfriend, the suspiciously perfect Toni), changed the game for me. Instead of feeling outside the group, I suddenly felt part of it.

The next day there was a chestnut party, or *castañada*, at the house of a painter called Bosco, uncle of Saskia's friend Lali. Bosco, bearded, bearlike, an anarchist, a great lover of women, preferably unclothed (he immediately asked Saskia to model for him), was like an amalgam of Picasso and Miró, or the epitome of a Catalan artist—earthy, sensual, slightly surreal, but also warm, unpretentious, and hospitable. His house, surrounded by a small olive grove, not far from the sea, had a definitive quality for me—definitive of Mediterranean simplicity and beauty, the kind of house I would like to live in if I ever grew up. It was distantly or not so distantly related to Horace's Sabine Farm.

Not much else about the castañada remains in my memory, except for a Horatian glimpse, of Bosco's daughter Ariadna, a shy seventeen-year-old beauty who later became an actress. Years later I had the chance to meet her again, at a theater party, but I backed out. Maybe I didn't want to tarnish the image I had of her as the perfect embodiment of a girl on the brink of adulthood,

curious, intrigued, half in, half out of the game. She could, perhaps, have been the young girl in one of Horace's most risqué
poems, the one that begins: "Why are you avoiding me, Chloe,
like a fawn following her timid mother over the pathless hills,
jittery with fear when the wind rustles the leaves?"

Anna became not just my friend but my guide to Catalan
culture, the holder of the thread to lead through that labyrinth. I
began to learn about what Catalans considered the long suppres-
sion of their culture and language, not just under Franco, when
speaking Catalan in public was forbidden, but time and again
through history. But once again it was learning not just about facts
but ways of being.

I suppose what was so good about Barcelona was the blend
of formal and informal learning. The formal part was happening
at the university where I had enrolled in the Diploma de Estu-
dios Hispánicos.

The course and the university were not immediately attractive; classes took the form of lectures given in Spanish in big
drafty nineteenth-century lecture halls, with seventy or so students taking notes, and rarely asking questions, in a style that
seemed as antiquated as the buildings and the furniture.

The University of Barcelona was not Cambridge University,
that was for sure; just a big, rather dingy neo-Gothic building
with a couple of dark courtyards, where stunted orange and
lemon trees struggled toward the sun, in the noisy dusty center
of the city, with no medieval colleges or dreaming spires or dreamy
gardens on the Backs, and the idea of a one-to-one tutorial as
remote as an audience with the Pope. It was a shock realizing
how a different history and political system could lead to such a
different outcome—a shock once again to confront my own privilege. My own college library at Cambridge was better than the
central library of Barcelona University.

But the course had its virtues. Just listening to lecturers
speaking in Spanish helped my comprehension; the teaching of

the language, conducted by the senior grammarian Francesc Marsá, was rigorous in a way I appreciated. Marsá's other course, Etnolinguística Hispana, was a gem; a fascinating, erudite explanation of the layers of history contained in words, of the evolution of the Spanish language, the Arab influence, the American influence, all illustrated with a humor as dry as fino sherry. Once Marsá paused in the middle of some ethnolinguistic discussion and remarked that he had recently visited England and been impressed by the quality of programming on the BBC. The experience had made him give thanks for the abysmal quality of Spanish TV: at least there was no temptation whatever to watch it.

I was glad also to be taking a course in history, in particular focusing on the background to Spain's twentieth-century tragedy, the Civil War, which I was also trying to understand via Gerald Brenan's great book *The Spanish Labyrinth*.

Most fertile of all was my introduction to Spanish literature; beginning to read short novels by Sender and Galdós, poetry by Lorca and Salinas.

The point—and here is the reconnection with Horace—is that I became penetrated and fertilized by another language, culture and poetry at the level of soul. I don't think I could have found my way back to Horace and to Latin poetry without this detour into the living Latinate language of Spanish; my own poetry never would have evolved the way it did, seeking and finding its greater emotional directness and expressiveness, without the benign influence of poetry written in Spanish, and, perhaps even more, of Spanish and Catalan people.

Seven

The Freedom of the Poet

For Horace the years immediately after Philippi were not easy. He had escaped from the carnage and confusion of the battle-field, but his life was still in danger. At some point he must have decided that the cause for which he had risked his life was a lost one. Others, including his close friends Messalla Corvinus and Pompeius Varus, would continue to fight with what was left of the Republican army under Sextus Pompeius. Horace must have decided to leave the east, where the especially vindictive Antony was hunting down and killing enemies of the triumvirate, and return to Italy, where conditions were somewhat safer.

In Italy Horace found that his father's property in Venusia had been confiscated. "Humbled, with wings clipped and deprived of paternal home and property, bold poverty impelled me into writing verses": this is how he describes his state after Philippi in the letter to Florus. The verses he is talking about are probably the Epodes, the early poems in iambic meters, more savage, even despairing, and brutally angry at times, less urbane and ironic than anything he would write later. But he also needed a job, and he found one as a *scriba quaestorius*, a sort of mid-ranking civil servant. It actually sounds like quite a comfortable quasi sinecure, but Horace of course had higher ambitions.

The great turning point in his life came through the good offices of his friends the poets Virgil and Varius, and then Maecenas,

Augustus's right-hand man and culture minister, the man who, as the young poet's patron, would take Horace under his wing, render his days blessed. This fateful meeting must have taken place in the early 30s B.C.

Winning the friendship of Maecenas, the most important single event in Horace's life, did not happen by chance, and it did not happen instantly: "When I came into your presence I stuttered out a few words; tongue-tied self-consciousness inhibited me from saying more. My story was not that I was the son of a famous father, not that I rode about my lands mounted on a splendid Saturian horse: I told you what I was. In your usual way, you said little in reply and I went away; then, nine months later, you sent for me again and asked me to join the circle of your friends."

Horace has not forgotten those nine months, which must have seemed quite long. But he is writing in exultant mood; even if the wider political freedom for which he fought at Philippi has not come to pass, he has been granted his personal economic freedom, the freedom to do and write what he likes, as he likes. "In the reign of the Divine Augustus," as Seneca says in *De beneficiis*, "men's words were not yet hazardous to them, though they could cause them difficulties."

In this same poem (the sixth satire of Book 1), one of the most revealing and joyous he ever wrote, Horace describes the life he is now able to lead. "Wherever my fancy takes me, I set out on my own. I ask the price of vegetables and flour; often at dusk I stroll around the Circus, full of hustlers, and the Forum. I have my fortune told; then it's back home for supper, my wholesome fare of leeks and peas and fritters."

It sounds even better in Latin (of course). "Quacumque libido est," incorporating the word Freud used for desire and sexual energy, sounds a bit stronger than "wherever the fancy leads." And "incedo solus" could be a buoyant motto for the whole of Horace's poetry. Yes, it means "I saunter forth alone" into the marketplace and the Circus and the Forum, but it also means "I set out alone," I follow my own path, a poetic path no one has trod before, as the first poet ever to bring the full range of Archaic Greek music and meter to Latin verse.

Horace considered himself a lucky man. His luck had begun with having an excellent father, not a sophisticated man, but a person of great shrewdness and wisdom, who had put everything he had earned (a considerable amount, clearly) into giving his gifted son the best education money could buy. Movingly, Horace says that he would not have swapped this father for any other in the world, even one much higher up the social scale. His luck had also included a series of escapes: most dramatically at Philippi, but also from a falling tree on his estate (a near miss he mentions so often one feels it must be a true story).

At a similar age, perhaps a few years older, I too felt I had fallen on my feet. I had escaped more metaphysical dangers than those which faced Horace—the melancholy and confusion I had suffered in my early twenties. Freelance journalism was coming my way in a steady enough stream—sufficient for living—while also providing time for other kinds of writing. Above all, I finally felt freed up to write poetry. Then I found a place that for a while brought reliable exhilaration and inspiration, and a poet cannot ask for more than that.

You turn right off the main Cádiz-Algeciras road just after the white village of Facinas and just before you reach the very southern tip of Spain. A small road climbs and winds through rough, rocky green fields, rising to a pass; from there you look down onto a magnificent broad bay, with a high headland on the right, and in the far distance, across the Strait of Gibraltar, the coast of Africa.

Once upon a time this was Baelo Claudia, a prosperous Roman port town noted for the production of garum, the paste made from rancid fish guts beloved of Roman emperors; perhaps Horace (if he was not a vegetarian) also had a taste for it. You can still see the well-preserved remains of a garum factory, together with a theater and other buildings.

Modern Bolonia is much less grand than Roman Baelo Claudia: a straggle of low, mostly one-story buildings; a hotel, a few hostels, a primary school. In the summer, or the weekends, it gets quite busy with day-trippers, but in January Bolonia is desolate, or wildly beautiful, according to taste. Horace was acquainted with just such a place, an out-of-the-way spot called Lebedus.

Why should a poet like such a place, which would be shunned by most normal people as intolerably dull? Let me give my reason, as Horace does not give his. A day in Bolonia begins with an early-morning walk along the mile-long beach of tawny sand, past the fenced enclosure of the ruins, gradually shaking off the cobwebs and the stiffness of the night, letting the remnants of strange dreams (I always dream intensely here) dissolve in the salty air. There will be waders, sanderlings, plovers, plying the wet foreshore, and terns and gannets plunging for fish in the bay. Every morning this beach is swept clean (or cleanish—all sorts of jetsam lands up here) by the tide; a tabula rasa, ready for the daily renewed act of creation.

Forty minutes pacing along the beach is enough to stir an appetite for breakfast. My favorite place to have breakfast in Bolonia is the dining room of the Hostal Ríos, looking out to the Atlantic past a small garden frequented by warblers and swallows. I sit here with my *tostada con mantequilla y mermelada* and my café con leche and my notebook, recording dreams, events of the previous days, the stirrings of poems.

I don't always feel like a poet. The visitations of the muses, as Horace would have put it, are not constant. Ah, muses, you might say, with an amused or ironic moue. Homer might have invoked his muse at the start of the *Odyssey*—"speak to me of that man, O muse!"—without too much self-consciousness, but surely muses thereafter became mere literary conventions or affectations.

Thinking of the way poems come to me makes me consider the way Horace speaks about the muses. Of course it was conventional to talk about muses in Horace's day, but that does not mean that it could not be at the same time deeply personal.

I'm thinking of a short poem that comes toward the end of Horace's first book of odes. It begins and ends with the muses. "A friend of the Muses, I will cast off sadness and fear—throw them to the wild winds to cart off into the Cretan sea." The Horace scholar and translator David West makes the opening even more emphatic: "I am a friend of the Muses." And then at the end Horace addresses a particular Muse, whom he calls Pimpleis— and the name probably sounded almost as strange to the Romans as it does to us—meaning the lady who comes from Pimpla near the Pierian fountain of the Muses on Mount Olympus. "O you who rejoice in unpolluted springs, weave sun-opened flowers into a crown for my friend Lamia, weave them, my sweet Pimpleis; without you nothing I make has any meaning."

Yes, the references are remote and erudite (and I repeat that they would have seemed quite remote and erudite even to Horace's original readers), but the strength and depth of personal feeling are unmistakable. This is a poem about poetry and the inspiration for poetry, about poetry's power to banish gloom and fear, and as in so many of his poems Horace locates that source and inspiration outside himself; locates it, in fact, in the divine.

There is a big truth here that is much more important than the small elucidations of scholars (which is not to say they are not important too). Poetry is not something that can be willed. Poetry is something that involves commerce with the divine. Poetry is something that wells up from the center of the earth, like the pure springs in Horace's poems, and which aspires toward the heavens, like the sun-opened flowers.

In Bolonia, I follow these Horatian precepts. I am there to gather images, as the bee gathers nectar.

The life I live there is more that of a Beat poet than a sophisticated Horatian. I have discovered, not far from Bolonia, a gathering place for alternative folk called the Galería de Arte Elemental, run by an implacably idealistic South African woman called Sheena, who lives with two architects, one Iranian and one Sardinian. From a small Andalusian farm building and a big thatched African hut they run an unlikely combination of art gallery, permaculture garden, café, and retreat.

Here, on one of those January days, feeling low and fluish with my inevitable January cold, I meet a shy, stubbly, bespectacled poet called Aiken, his Chilean friend Coco, who is a kind of clown, and Coco's doe-eyed German girlfriend, Ilse. After lunch and some weeding in the permaculture garden I drive them over to Bolonia. The time we spend there could stand for many other Bolonia times.

Big breakers are creaming shoreward in the still air. There's a hazy afternoon sun. I've made friends with a tawny, slightly goofy dog called Rufo, and we throw sticks and stones for him.

We have a drink in the Bar Ríos and then outside another bar, Las Rejas, Coco notices a dead tabby cat that's been there for days. He's determined to bury the cat, with honors, borrows a spade, and sets to digging in the hard earth. An old man is watching us; laughing a bit, he says to me, "What your friend is doing is well done." He suggests putting up a cross.

Later on we decide to barbecue a chicken. I still have the price of the chicken, bought in Facinas, written down in my notebook: 972 pesetas, which seems a lot. At some point in the proceedings I give the car keys to Coco and Aiken to go to buy wood while I wait in a bar. They appear to be taking an awfully long time. Suspicions form in my mind, but on balance I tell myself it was a good thing to do, to give them the car keys; the kind of thing a tough guy does in a Western.

"Thought we'd sold the car, right?" says Aiken when they eventually reappear. We head off for Coco's house in the hills. You have to drive up an almost impassable track, park the car in a small meadow, and walk farther up a path through boulders, all in the dark.

Coco's house has no electricity or running water; we light candles; I chop chorizo, tomato, and onion to make salad. Coco launches into a story of a summer romance: "She was so perfect, man, she was too perfect, perfect fucking legs, perfect butt, that was why it had to end. I felt she was the woman I wanted to work with, to study with, to live with. I wrote letters, I put everything into those letters, and she writes back with what—the weather in Italy. I mean come on, man."

Then there's trouble lighting the fire; the smoke keeps blowing back into the room. But the barbecued chorizo and chicken pieces, when they come, are good; we wash them down with a bottle of Romeral rioja (300 pesetas).

The talk is all about women. "If you go looking for a relationship, you won't find one," says Aiken finally, a beautifully constructed dam to stem Coco's torrents of angst. By the time I leave, the moon, full three days before, is just appearing over the crags behind Coco's house. Coco and Aiken light me down with a candle lamp. I will never see them again.

So what was the point of all that—of all those Bolonia days and nights, of the wanderings along the beach picking up poetic jetsam? It might sound supremely aimless, and so it was. At some level you need to surrender yourself to aimlessness to write poetry. Horace implied as much when he said "I set out alone." That could be the great poetic manifesto, echoed two thousand years later by Yeats's "I will arise and go now, and go to Innisfree." Why go to Innisfree? An island in a lake in the middle of nowhere?

Rumors reach Bolonia. A whale has been washed up on the beach. I decide to go to see it, too late as usual.

When I get there I find the municipal authorities in attendance. The decaying, foul-smelling whale carcass has become a health hazard. A JCB digger is trying hopelessly to bury the great slobbering mound of putrescent flesh. Out of this comes my poem "Whale Burial," which is not just about the burial of a whale, but about the fate of poetry, an enormity. And could there be just a hint of an unconscious tribute to Horace, or Flaccus as he was known to friends, in the first word?

WHALE BURIAL

Flaccid, beyond recognition,
your soft remains are littered on the beach.

Flung up on this coast between continents
a week ago, you had form and substance.

People came to inspect
your unearthly proportions.

Once a generation such a marvel happens;
you give names to places.

You began to dry and rot
simultaneously.

You sagged and aged,
a ship-sized bag of bones and juices.

Downwind it smelled like a fish factory;
but you retained vestiges of yourself.

Now the dissolution has gone too far:
it has become a public nuisance.

A small army of men, the burial party,
a grave as big as a house.

The earth-scooper scrabbles ineffectually,
trying to grasp your slippery secretions.

It speads you out farther and deeper.

Parts of you seep into the sand,
membranous sacs of blood and semen.

Your skeleton is distributed
among the people.

Your jaws will be rejoined as an arch
through which air and pilgrims pass.

Your penis will be hung up in a bar,
a lewd and leathery baton.

No reliquary can hold your bones,
but still I am thinking of that beach,

and those men, too many for the job,
staring, with their hands in their pockets,

at an enormity.

Eight

Love, Friendship, Therapy

I would have got nowhere without friendships; that has been part of my luck, a very big part in the informal world of freelance journalism. I like to think that I have not just been lucky in my friendships; friendships need nurturing and cultivating too. I believe Horace would have said the same; no writer has ever cultivated friendships, and celebrated friendship, so assiduously, both in his own time and in future time.

This is the way he presents himself: Horace is your reliable friend. Whatever the weather, he will invite you in. If it is winter, and somehow it often is, there will be a warm fire, logs ablaze. A suitable bottle of wine will be opened, perhaps more than one. And as the wine flows, so will the conversation. There will be reminiscences (you have known each other a long time); talk about the old days, love, and life.

That is the seductive promise. Somehow Horace more than any other writer has lured his readers down this primrose path of imagining that a long-dead writer could be their familiar. The roll call of those who have counted Horace as their friend includes Petrarch (who wrote a long and fulsome letter to him in Latin), Voltaire, the mathematician and philosopher the Marquis de Condorcet (who had a copy of the Odes with him in his prison cell when he died, a victim of Robespierre's purges), Wordsworth, Nietzsche, Brecht—not just the more obvious Horatians: Ben

Jonson, Andrew Marvell, John Dryden, Alexander Pope, Samuel
Johnson, W. H. Auden, Louis MacNeice.

Voltaire's verse epistle to Horace begins like this:

> I've lived longer than you; my poetry will have a shorter
>   life.
> But as I approach my grave I am going to put all my
>   efforts
> Into following the lessons of your philosophy—
> Into despising death and savoring the taste of life,
> Into reading your writings full of grace and good sense
> As one drinks an old wine which makes one feel young.

So far so good. Voltaire's tone is genuinely affectionate, and humble, and true to Horace's spirit, even if you might detect just a
trace of condescension in that phrase "full of grace and good
sense." Isn't that just a little too comfortable? But the image of
the old wine is perfect.

Then Voltaire goes on, banging his own drum too loudly:

> Your maxims and your verses,
> Your spirit dedicated to justice and truth, your
>   contempt for hell,
> All of that convinces me that Horace died an honest
>   man:
> The least citizen in Rome died like that:
> There, you would never see the Abbe Griset
> Tormenting a sick man in the name of Eternal God.

Hasn't Voltaire lost touch just a bit with Horace here, conscript-
ing him to an anticlerical cause that sounds too militant and
certain for the skeptical Horace?

A near contemporary of Voltaire was the English poet Alexander Pope—surely one of the truest and best friends Horace

had in the afterlife? Pope, after all, more or less based his writing life on Horace. Pope revived Horace's form of the verse epistle; modeled his "Essay on Criticism" on Horace's *Ars Poetica*, and in that work wrote these words:

> Horace . . .
> Will, like a friend, familiarly convey
> The truest notions in the easiest way.

Familiarity seems to have bred something like contempt. Horace doesn't sound like a true friend in this passage, but like a slick but deadly boring conveyor of truisms. There is in fact something subtly wrong with Pope's all-too-easy assimilation of Horace as a good Augustan chap. There is something wrong at a philosophical level, a misunderstanding about the nature of truth and poetry.

Pope's words imply that true notions already exist somewhere, before being put into writing. Elsewhere in a more famous line he speaks of "what oft was thought but ne'er so well expressed." In this version, poetry is like finery draped on a statue. What is so wrong with it was beautifully expressed by Maurice Merleau-Ponty in an unpublished text written at the very end of his life: "Language is never the mere clothing of a thought which otherwise possesses itself in full clarity. The meaning of a book is given . . . not so much by its ideas as by [an] . . . accent, this particular modulation of speech."

Even more beautifully, in Proust's *À l'ombre des jeunes filles en fleurs*, Elstir says this: "One does not receive wisdom; one must discover it oneself after a journey which no one can make for us, or spare us the trouble of, because it consists in its essence of a point of view on things."

There are good reasons why Horace attracts posthumous friends like no other poet. Horace put friendship at the center of his poetry. Horace did not just make friendship a theme of his poetry, he put his poetry within the frame of friendship. The characteristic mode of the Odes is the address to a friend— Maecenas above all, Virgil, Postumus, Pompeius, or Licinius; the Epistles are letters to friends, or acquaintances; the Satires too are often friendly dialogues.

Friendship is the context, almost the environment of Horace's poetry. Friendship means conversation; it often means conviviality, the sharing not just of words and thoughts and feelings but of food and wine, the winter view. It means a sustained warmth, not a passing fancy; it means frankness, not flattery.

Once again I can hear the voice of the scholar, suggesting this is just another literary trope, or warning that friendship did not mean quite the same thing to Romans that it does to us. Well of course friendship is a literary trope to Horace, and *amicitia* can mean the relationship of client to patron, but it is also much more than that. When Horace says "amicus" he can mean something remarkably like what we mean by "friend." The people Horace addresses his poems to are mostly real; he had real relationships with them, even if the relationship within the poem is fictive.

In Book 1 of Horace's Satires there is a remarkably modern-seeming travel poem, or travelogue in the form of a poem, that tells the story of a journey Horace made in 37 B.C. from Rome to the heel of Italy, complete with country inns, barges, woodsmoke, gnats, frogs, and a frustrated erotic encounter. This is Slow Travel avant la lettre. Fast travel hadn't yet been invented.

The best day of the trip, Horace tells us, was the one when three friends, Plotius and his two fellow poets, Varius and Virgil, turned up to meet Horace and his party at a place called Sinuessa. There were so many hugs and rejoicings. There was the merriment, if that's the word, of friendship—the best thing in the world, according to Horace.

I believe Horace really did think friendship was, taken all in all, the best thing in the world. There is no prouder boast in his poetry than this one, also from the Satires: "I live in the affection of my friends." The Latin words "vivo carus amicis" mean literally "I live dear to my friends."

This wasn't such a strange view; Aristotle, after all, in the *Nicomachean Ethics*, had said that friendship was one of the things in the world human beings could least afford to be without. Does friendship mean male friendship, for Horace? So it would seem, but Horace surely had the potential to be a good friend of women too. There's a poem in which he begins by cursing the falling tree on his estate that nearly killed him, and the man who planted it. He then goes on to imagine what would have happened if he had not been so lucky, if instead of scrambling back home he had paid the ferryman. The first person Horace encounters in the Underworld is a female poet strumming her lyre. She is Sappho, the greatest woman poet of antiquity, best known to us because of her frank love of women, but known and revered by Horace as the poet who opened up once and for all the realm of the personal in poetry. There is no one he would rather see or hear; she is, in that sense, his greatest friend.

It is not such a surprising thing for a philosopher to say that friendship is the most important human requirement, but it is a much more unusual thing for a poet to say. We expect something more, or more heated, from poetry than friendship. We expect passion. When I think about poets' relationships, I might think about Sappho's intense yearnings for the women she loved, or about Catullus's tortured affair with Clodia, about Dante's love for the unattainable Beatrice, about Shakespeare's complicated love triangle in the Sonnets, about Keats and Fanny Brawne, about Baudelaire and his "black Venus" Jeanne Duval, about Verlaine and Rimbaud, about Yeats and Maud Gonne, about Ted Hughes and Sylvia Plath. I don't really think about friendships. Friendships seem more suitable for prose. Even Tennyson's friendship with Hallam, which produced "In Memoriam," seems more like a love affair.

This deliberate turning down of the heat, if that is what it is, tends to put young readers off Horace. It put me off. I wanted white-hot passion, so I gravitated toward Catullus. I wanted a poet who could say like Catullus, "I hate and love."

No mistaking the passion there, the exultancy, the excitement of possession, the agony and bitterness of jealousy, betrayal, and loss. As schoolboys we sniggered over the rude bits ("pedicabo vos et irrumabo"), but the erotic passion registered as much as the graphic sex.

No one could doubt that the sequence of poems Catullus wrote to the lover he called Lesbia, whom most scholars assume to have been the aristocrat Clodia Metelli, referred to a real love affair. What young person could fail to respond to a poem that goes like this?

> let's live my lesbia live and love
> not give a fuck for all the stuff-
> y stupid strictures of old men
> suns may sink and rise again
> when death snuffs out our candle's light
> there's nothing left but endless night
> give me a thousand kisses then a hun-
> dred, then a thousand more, and then
> a second hundred and a thou
> yet another hundred and now
> we'll have piled up too huge a sum
> to count or know and we'll keep dumb
> so no ill-intentioned schmuck
> can envy us our blessed luck

This was a love that colored everything, about which you could say with John Donne seventeen hundred years later "nothing else is." I suppose that was the kind of love I wanted then, even though Catullus himself could have warned about the dire consequences.

Then there was Propertius, whom we glanced at, who made his mistress, not the emperor, the center of everything—surely the choice any young man of mettle should make, the choice the members of the Bloomsbury Group would have applauded. (E. M. Forster: "If I had to choose between betraying my country and betraying my friend, I hope I should have the guts to betray my country.") But not the choice Horace made. And then Ovid, the cool erotic gamester, the poet who says, let's look at love as a game and play it for all it's worth.

Horace's dealings with Eros seemed indirect. His love poems, such as they are, tend to be ironic, humorous, lewd rather than passionate. Only very occasionally, as in the first ode of Book 4, does he let down his guard and reveal the intensity he usually masks.

For the most part Horace offers, or accepts, only the glancing blows of love, not the full-on assault of Catullus or Propertius.

That does not mean, I now see—though it has taken me decades to see this—that he is either heartless or indifferent. In fact it could mean quite the reverse.

Horace is guarded about love. But someone might have reason to be guarded. He might feel that the moment in which he let down his guard would be fatal. That is certainly the case for the gladiator, to whom Horace compares himself in one of his last love poems.

Maybe Horace's social position made him especially insecure, especially guarded. He was already, constantly, on his guard about that, about the jibes directed against "the son of a freed slave." Maybe something even further back had made him more deeply guarded, emotionally—the loss of his mother, whom he never mentions?

The one thing he wanted to be, above all, was free. After all his father's struggles at least the son could achieve that, to be "in thrall to no master." Or no mistress. On no account would he become his lover's slave (except, of course, that he would find himself contradicting himself; very well, I contradict myself).

And that, precisely, was what Catullus and Propertius, and before them Sappho, had become.

The posture of the love elegist is one of abasement, emotional if not physical. The love elegist opens himself or herself up to every imaginable wound or sadistic attack from the beloved. And that is something Horace is not prepared to suffer—or to let the reader see him suffer.

At the most we will see those glancing blows. But the glancing blows give away so much.

One thing Horace certainly isn't is a romantic love poet. His earliest love poems, in the collection he called Epodes, are quite strikingly nasty and brutal. Here's how one (Epode 8) begins:

> The idea of you complaining
> All this long and tedious time
> That I'm insufficiently virile
> When you look yourself in the mirror
> And see one black stump of a tooth
> A forehead gouged with wrinkles
> And that gaping hole
> Between shriveled buttocks
> Like a cow's with diarrhea!

You could find this funny, or quite disturbing. I wonder whether Horace isn't getting in some kind of preemptive strike, a wounding by invective so severe as to prevent any rejoinder. Though perhaps the kind of woman he seems to be describing here would be fully capable of answering back, of giving him as good as he deals out.

One of the glancing blows or hints he allows in the Odes is

an allusion to a stormy relationship with "slave-born Myrtale, fiercer than the wild winds of the Adriatic when they howl in towards Calabria, who when a better love beckoned held me happily chained." This is the way the mature Horace does love, elliptical, compressing a whole novel into four lines. That last phrase is one of Horace's most pregnant, "grata compede" in Latin, literally "with pleasing fetter." Pregnant and also uncomfortable, in its graphic reference to the physical paraphernalia of slavery. And just before, to describe Myrtale, Horace has used the word "libertina," slave-born, the same word he uses again and again of his own father.

Octavio Paz, in his beautiful and thought-provoking study of love in Western culture, *The Double Flame*, dismisses Horace's love poems as "variations . . . on the traditional themes of eroticism." In other words, just commonplaces, however beautifully wrought. Is this fair? Or could Paz be falling victim to the common misconception that because everyone after Horace refashioned his tropes, Horace's originals sound like commonplaces?

The first love poem in the Odes, Odes 1.5, addressed to Pyrrha, may sound conventional. It was translated by the young John Milton, or rather as he put it "rendered almost word for word, without rhyme, according to the Latin measure, as near as the language will permit." Milton set down the Latin text beside his translation, whether to show his youthful confidence and bravado, in tackling one of the stiffest poetic challenges he could set himself, or to show, after all, the impossibility of the task, we shall never know.

THE FIFTH ODE OF HORACE, LIB 1

What slender youth, bedewed with liquid odours,
Courts thee on roses in some pleasant cave,
    Pyrrha? For whom bind'st thou
    In wreaths thy golden hair,

Plain in thy neatness? Oh, how oft shall he
On faith and changed gods complain, and seas
 Rough with black winds and storms
 Unwonted shall admire,
Who now enjoys thee credulous, all gold;
Who always vacant, always amiable,
 Hope thee, of flattering gales
 Unmindful! Hapless they
To whom thou untried seem'st fair! Me, in my vowed
Picture, the sacred wall declares to have hung
 My dank and dropping weeds
 To the stern God of Sea.

Milton certainly captures, as very few English translators have done, the terseness and compactness of the original. There are some successful touches, as you would expect from a master poet—"all gold," "my dank and dropping weeds." And some less successful ones: surely "plain in thy neatness" is far too Puritan for the cavalier Pyrrha? But the real problem is that Milton has created a sterile hybrid—something that by sticking too close to the Latin fails to live in English.

Here's something more contemporary:

Who's making love to you now, Pyrrha,
 What beautiful boy drenched
 In Pour Homme and rose petals in a cave,
Who are you binding your blonde tresses for,

So artfully simple? Soon he'll be looking
 Out to sea, cursing fickle promises and gods,
 Gazing out amazed at the breakers,
The winds whipping them up to fury;

Yes, the boy who thinks he has you now, all gold,

Who hopes you'll always be like this,
　All his, biddable and available; who has
No idea of the treacherous change of breeze.

Oh I pity those whose image of you
　Shines untarnished—who've never tried you.
　As for me, I've come back safe from
Drowning; I've a healthy respect for the sea.

Pyrrha probably didn't exist, in the way that Catullus's Lesbia and Propertius's Cynthia existed. But the fact that she may be a fictional character doesn't make her unreal, any more than Natasha Rostova or Anna Karenina or Emma Bovary is unreal. Pyrrha is a brilliant fictional creation, sketched with Horace's usual extreme economy, unforgettable, because those details, the blonde hair done up in that artfully simple way, the tremendous word "aurea," golden (she is the original golden girl), are etched with such precise beauty.

What a superb poem this is, which simultaneously holds and burnishes the image of this treacherous golden girl, quite irresistibly attractive—and what the future will bring for her lover, and then for the others outside the pairing, which at the start seems so glamorously exclusive, and then for the poet himself, who has been through this, or something like this, who has come through unscathed.

As usual with Horace, he is both in and out of the game, as Whitman would put it, much later, and rather more out than in. For some readers, for most young readers, that will make this kind of Horatian love poem a less compelling, absorbing experience, than the very different kind of love poem offered by Catullus or Propertius.

But the more you look at this complex and masterly poem, the less conventional, the more Cubist it seems. Horace's love poetry may unsettle us because it is multiperspectival; it is not content always to look at love from one perspective, the obsessively close focus of the besotted lover. The "I" of this poem is not the heroic lover but the man who has escaped love, the man who hangs up his dripping garments to the sea god, in an ironic gesture.

Unsettling, more precisely, are the abrupt shifts in perspective, first from the idyllic love cave strewn with roses to the bleak seashore, and then from the single betrayed lover to a whole string of others, and then to the poet, deflating any romantic mood with his impersonation of a wet blanket.

The Pyrrha ode, which opens so seductively, ends, as so often with Horace, in a rueful recognition of reality. But Horace isn't always an amatory curmudgeon.

Four odes after the Pyrrha ode comes the Soracte ode, the poem that first converted me to Horace, which set this whole long slow train in motion. The Soracte ode is not in any normal sense a love poem. It seems more a convivial poem, one of those Horace poems set in the warm—never overheated—context of friendship and wine and the natural world. But the shifts of perspective that in the Pyrrha ode lead away from love, or any simple-minded conception of love, here lead surprisingly toward it.

The poem, which begins in winter, with a description of a snowcapped mountain that is also an image of aging, of the white hair on the crown, shifts in a series of unlikely key changes to summer and youth, and from the country outside Rome to Rome itself. In the wonderful final image, of the giggling girls in the corner of the square, and the love token snatched from a finger that only feigns resistance, there is nothing ironic at all.

Horace may be too old for this kind of thing, but he urges his friend (a friend who may be as fictitious as Pyrrha) to go for it, not to resist the honey sweetness of young love, and all the dancing. It's a magnificently generous ending to a magnificently generous poem.

Is Horace really too old for love, past it, a has-been? Of

course not. Suetonius in his *Life of Horace* says that the poet was "immoderately lustful," and cites a report (which may well be discounted as Roman celebrity gossip) that "in a room lined with mirrors the poet had prostitutes posed so that whichever way he looked he saw a reflection of lust." (Silvio Berlusconi, eat your heart out.) Returning from the realms of fantasy to reality, we can state that he wrote the first three books of odes in his mid-to late thirties and very early forties, a time of life we consider still young, though perhaps for the Romans it represented early middle age.

Horace may not be a young lover anymore, and he may in the Pyrrha ode and the Soracte ode look back on young love with different attitudes, of gratitude to have escaped from all that madness, and of gentle nostalgia and regret, but he can still be a different kind of lover. He can offer mature love.

This is what he is doing in the ode that comes four odes after the Soracte ode, addressed to a certain Lydia whose youthful and rather violent passion for young Telephus is making the middle-aged poet jealous, sad, and angry. He is sad and angry not for himself, mind you, but for Lydia and the fact that her delicate, vulnerable beauty is subject to such rude assaults.

What Horace proposes instead is something that, alas, is highly unlikely to convince Lydia in the heat of her passion. The poem ends with a profoundly moving image of the felicity that comes to those whose love survives, not torn apart by bitter quarreling, until their dying day (with poetic license he seems to imagine both perishing on the same day):

> The real deep happiness comes from this:
> An unbroken bond that survives all quarrels,
> That keeps two close until the final day.

Probably Horace did not get the girl, but he left us something for all time.

A bit middle-aged, a bit staid? Yes, maybe. Cautious, certainly. If Horace is cautious about love, that is in part because he recognizes that love is a god, just as strong a god as the great Mississippi River in T. S. Eliot's "The Dry Salvages," if not so sullen.

The god or goddess of love has a name; her name is Venus, and Horace repeatedly refers to her throughout the Odes. She is perhaps his second-favorite deity, after his favorite, his very own personal god, Mercury. And in one of the shortest and apparently slightest of the Odes, the companion piece of the longer invocation to Mercury, Horace invokes the goddess of love.

TO VENUS (ODES 1.30)

Venus, queen of Paphos and Cnidos,
Abandon your love-island of Cyprus, come
Here to the shrine of Glycera who
Summons you with incense.

Make sure the burning boy who stokes desire
Is with you, and the Nymphs and Graces, half-
　　undressed,
And Youth, so ugly without you, and my
Own god, Mercury.

It's a poem that seems to bring out the worst in scholars; they want to insist that it is derivative, an imitation of a fragment by Sappho or an epigram by Posidippus, or a deeply unattractive exercise in cynicism in which Mercury becomes the pimp for a courtesan called Glycera.

Eduard Fraenkel, on the other hand, called it "a little poem, a perfect creation," which is true, as far as it goes. And one can go even further; this little poem is actually a prayer, and it contains Horace's deep feelings about how he wanted love to be—that is, as the sympathetic Horace scholar David West has put it, "passionate, uninhibited, gracious, joyous." The mention of Mercury at the end is there for two reasons: first, as a sort of signature, linking love to Horace, and second, to bring the mercurial qualities Horace so treasured, of eloquence and playfulness and humor, into the arena of love. One of the aspects of love Horace captures exceptionally well is its unexpectedness, its surprisingness, its capacity of always catching you unawares. One of the ways love can surprise you is by reigniting a flame you thought had died. This is the subject of a lovely ode in the third book.

DONEC GRATUS ERAM TIBI (ODES 3.9)

"In those days when you fancied me,
When there was no one you'd rather throw
Your lovely arms around, I felt as strong
And happy as the Emperor of India."

"In those days when you had the hots
For me, and Lydia was top of the pops,
Not upstart Chloe, I felt strong
And heroic as Queen Boudicca."

"My latest love is Chloe, from Salonica,
Brilliant poetess and handy lutenist;
She's so gorgeous that I'd happily
Die for her, so long as she survived."

"My new boyfriend's name is Calais,
The son of Thurian Ornytus; let me tell you
It's a mutual passion, and I'd die
Twice for him, so long as he was spared."

> "What if the old flame rekindled; brought
> Parted lovers back together?
> What if fair-haired Chloe got the shove,
> And Lydia could walk in through an open door?"

> "He's drop-dead beautiful; you're hopelessly
> Unstable, worse than a storm at sea;
> All the same you're the one I really want
> To live with, until our day is done."

For me two qualities in particular emanate from this poem. First, it's a rare example in the annals of love poetry of sexual equality. The voices of the male and female lover are perfectly balanced not just in the number of lines but in the weight of sentiment. How rarely, when you think about it, in most love poetry (and that goes equally for poetry written by male and female love poets) do you hear the voice of the Other, the one the poem is addressed to, the one the poem is supposedly all about?

The second quality is also pretty rare in love poetry; it is the quality of humor, not strained I find, but delightfully warm and wry. You can't really imagine humor breaking into the dialogues of most of the great lovers of later Western literature; the humor or irony in the love affairs of Troilus and Cressida, or Romeo and Juliet, or Tristan and Isolde, comes from outside.

Horace, among his other failings, has been fingered as a chauvinist, maybe the most egregious chauvinist among all the Latin love poets. His unsparing poems about aging women are certainly cruel: psychoanalytically you might guess they contained an element of projection, of Horace's projecting his own unacceptable fears and feelings about aging and being unattractive onto a series of women. But which of the other Latin love poets, apart from Virgil, in his great portrayal of Dido, the crowning achievement of the *Aeneid*, gives so much voice, so many of the best lines, to his female lovers?

The greatest, most moving love poem Horace wrote comes in the third book of odes just two poems after the wry dialogue between the poet and Lydia. The ode begins with a beautiful invocation to the lyre that is about the power of poetry to tame wild things, to soften the heart of a wild girl in particular; but it lives for its magnificent dramatic conclusion, the closest Horace ever came to the world of Greek tragedy.

This conclusion tells the story, and gives us the words, of Hypermnestra, a singular figure in Greek mythology. Hypermnestra's nobility and generosity shine out in one of the darkest, bloodiest tales to be found even in that compendium of horrors. The fifty daughters of Danaus are forced to marry their cousins, the fifty sons of Danaus's brother Aegyptus. Danaus orders them to stab their husbands during their wedding night; all but one obey.

Here are the words Hypermnestra addresses to her newly wed husband (and you cannot doubt from Horace's account that the brief marriage has been joyfully consummated) as she urges him to escape:

"Get up, get up" she said to the young man lying there,
Her husband; "get up, before a longer sleep, the kind
You never wake from, comes from a place you'd not
    suspect:
Beware my murderous sisters and your father-in-law:

My sisters who like lionesses when they see a calf
Are ripping—each her own—their men apart;
I am kinder than they are, and I will not strike
You, dear, nor will I keep you under lock and key;

My father can torture me and throw me into chains
Because I pitied you and spared you, my own man;
I know my fate; he'll exile me, he'll ship me off
As far as ships can carry me, to Africa.

Go now, go: run like the wind, go where your footsteps
Take you; because it's night and we've made love,
Go with the following breeze, and be lucky,
And remember me and write my epitaph."

Not a word from the male lover, from Hypermnestra's husband,
Lynceus, you notice. He is too stunned, too amazed, too postco-
ital. She speaks for both of them, in one of the most moving and
generous love speeches in the whole of ancient literature. And
again it's a highly unusual moment in the annals of love. Love,
and love poetry, are so often, so overwhelmingly, about wanting
to have, to possess: Be here for me, now. But the strongest word
in all this marvelous speech is the littlest, the littlest word you
could imagine or find in Latin, or any language, the word that
consists of one letter, one vowel—*i*, the Latin for "go," second-
person singular imperative (the plural would be "ite," as in "ite,
missa est," the last words of the Roman liturgy). And no accident
that it was in this magnificent image of love as letting go, as the
giving rather than the taking of freedom, that Horace's Mercurial eloquence reached its greatest height.

The Hypermnestra ode may be Horace's greatest love
poem, but it is not his most personal. Hypermnestra, the Roman Juliet, is a figure quite far removed from him in every way.
And Horace does not like to give too much away, which is why
the first ode of Book 4 is such a remarkable poem. Once again
surprise comes into it: surprise that the superannuated poet-
lover, who swears he's past it, is still susceptible to the love goddess; surprise also, at least to some, that the object of love is
a boy.

At least as far as his poetry goes, Horace makes no distinction between boys and girls as objects of desire. This "bisexual-
ity" no doubt caused all sorts of discomfort to those living in
times when unconventional versions of sexuality were considered

sinful; it was certainly never mentioned by our classics teachers, who effected a kind of bowdlerization of the material they were teaching by simply not talking about the sexual content.

One way of putting this is that since the researches of Michel Foucault and his followers, we have learned to regard Horace and other ancient writers not as bisexual or homosexual but as presexual: that is, as living in a time that predates the modern notions of sexuality that were constructed in the seventeenth and eighteenth centuries. Another, rather simpler way of putting it is to say, with the psychoanalyst and literary critic Adam Phillips, that "we are all bisexual in dreams." Strictly speaking, I think Foucault goes deeper than Phillips: it is less true to say that in dreams we are all bisexual than that in dreams we revert to an older way of being or stratum of consciousness in which categories such as bisexual do not apply.

As a schoolboy at Eton in the 1970s I might as well have been living in pre-Freudian, let alone pre-Foucauldian times. I felt deeply ashamed of my homoerotic urges, which were shared by many if not most of my contemporaries. At sixteen I was rather pleasurably confused by being attracted to the full, ripe, womanly body of an eighteen-year-old friend of my sister's, who went with me to a Prom performance of Bruckner's Fifth Symphony. None of this would have surprised Horace, who admits in one of his satires to "a thousand passions for girls, a thousand for boys"; what would have surprised him is the deep shame felt for something entirely natural.

LOVE'S LATE RETURN (ODES 4.1)

Your orders are, to shake my sword,
  My rusty sword and trusty shield,
My gladiator's kit of long ago:
  Oh leave off, love goddess, please!

I'm not the man I used to be
   In good Lucinda's lambent reign.
At fifty plus the edge is off:
   I no longer rise to your challenges.

Push off, tigress, you and your cute
   Retinue of Cupids; let them
Aim their bows elsewhere—for instance
   Here's a perfect candidate:

Mister very promising barrister,
   Armed with bulging client list:
Grant him dearest heart's desire
   And he'll build you a brand-new shrine.

As for me I'm off the pace—
   You laugh, I swear, it's all too true—
Beyond the pull of woman's face,
   Or boy's: far out, far out at sea

Without the two-oared boat of hope,
   That endlessly renewing hope
That somewhere, some fine summer's day
   Will bring the perfect mesh of minds.

I'm past it, past the stage of all-
   Night drinking bouts, the last
One standing crowned with ivy wreaths
   Or coronets. So why, my boy,

Oh why, alas, are my cheeks wet
   With weeping from long dried-out eyes?
What's the sudden tongue-tiedness
   In all my floods of eloquence?

In dreams, at night, I hold you, dear,
    Tight in my arms; and then you're gone,
Running full tilt over lawns,
    Plunging in water, turned away from me.

I see this, perhaps Horace's most unguarded love poem, not so much as a homoerotic poem but as a poem about the elusiveness of desire, the ultimate ungraspability of the object of desire, a poem that looks forward to Proust and Jacques Lacan and Luis Buñuel.

Once again I underrated and mistook Horace. In some ways he is far less conventional and more subversive as a love poet than those radicals Catullus and Propertius. What he subverts is a romantic cult of love, of love as a religion (as Simon May has recently argued) that has survived Nietzsche's "death of God."

Having long wished he would be more committed, more passionate, more Catullus-like in his love poetry, I now see Horace as an essential anti-inflammatory in the West's overheated discourse on love. Horace offers the antidote to Wagner's *Tristan und Isolde*—to the compelling idea of love as Liebestod, that is of love so immense and all-embracing that it can only be consummated in death.

But there's no doubt that if forced to choose between love and friendship, Horace would have chosen friendship. Perhaps friendship tends to seem more important, and eros less overwhelmingly so, as one moves into middle age. Horace is unusual in having valued friendship so highly even when he was young.

There was a practical element to all this. Horace owed his life, that is to say the life that enabled him to write poetry, the life of *otium* rather than *negotium*, to friendship. One of the exemplary friendships between poets in all of history is that between Horace and Virgil.

Virgil and Horace were in many ways opposites—one from

the north of Italy, near Mantua, the son of a farmer, tall, dark, melancholic, shy, diffident, the other from Venusia in the south, the son of a freed slave, short, round, irascible, convivial. But the two must have become friends sometime after the battle of Philippi in 42 B.C., when both lost their paternal property, confiscated and given to his veterans by Octavian, soon to become Augustus. Virgil made these confiscations the theme of his first, immensely popular book of poems, the Eclogues; Horace hardly ever mentions them.

Horace never forgot the debt he owed to Virgil for the introduction Virgil gave him to his patron, Maecenas. In the sixth satire of Book 1, addressed to Maecenas, Horace sets it out in words of great simplicity and nobility: "I could not say I was blessed by chance, that it was pure luck that made me your friend. It was no chance that brought me to you; it was Virgil, the best of all men, and then after him Varius, who told you about me, what kind of man I was."

It took a special kind of friend to convey to Maecenas "what kind of man" Horace was. "Quid essem" ("essem" is the imperfect subjunctive of the verb "to be") in Latin has the echo of the English word "essence." Virgil and, later, Varius were able to convey to Maecenas the essence of Horace, his deepest being, his true quality, as man and poet. Maybe the short, round freedman's son did not look the part of a great poet; maybe he still had traces of a southern accent. But the quality was there; the inside was pure gold, and Maecenas recognized it.

The friendship of Virgil and Horace, which we know about only from Horace's side, is intriguing as much because of the differences as the similarities between them. These differences are beautifully suggested in two odes Horace addressed to his friend.

The first is cast as a warning to Virgil as he sets out on a perilous voyage to Greece. Horace begs the ship to return Virgil safe and sound from the shores of Attica. He puts it even more strongly than that: he says, "Please keep safe one half of my soul."

But is this about a literal voyage? Could it be a veiled warning about something else, about Virgil's perilous venture of embarking on an epic poem, modeled after the Greek Homer? Virgil's decision to compose the great Roman epic, urged by Maecenas and Augustus, marked a poetic parting of the ways between the two men.

Horace would never depart from the principle laid down by the Alexandrian Greek poet Callimachus: "big book, big mistake." He would carry on until he put down his pen for the last time, writing short or shortish poems. Virgil, not without huge misgivings, had broken the Callimachean rule, and the consequences might be grave.

In fact they were grave: Virgil agonized over the *Aeneid*, that most ambivalent of apologies for empire, and died, returning ironically enough from a journey to Greece undertaken with Augustus, before he could finish the epic to his satisfaction. He asked that the manuscript be destroyed at his death; his last wishes were countermanded by his literary executors, no doubt acting under the instructions of Augustus.

Perhaps Virgil's own justification, to himself, for writing the *Aeneid*—a poem about war and empire written by a man who had always celebrated peace, the harmony between man and the natural world, epitomized by an agriculture that respected the cosmos—was that he was writing for the losers as much as for the winners.

"There are tears for things; the travails of mortals do not go unwept." This is the most famous line in the *Aeneid*, or in the whole of Latin literature, beginning in Latin with the three words "sunt lacrimae rerum," and it could be the whole poem's motto. The poet's role is to shed the tears, to feel the sympathy for the losers, that humanize the blood, sweat, toil of empire building.

For that reason Virgil makes his hero Aeneas the most tearful epic hero in the history of poetry. On nearly every page of the epic the hero seems to be weeping; he weeps for the fall of his city, Troy, and he weeps again when he sees scenes from the Trojan War depicted on the walls of the temple of Juno in Carthage. He weeps as he obeys the gods' orders to leave his lover, Dido—by far the most sympathetic, tragic figure in the entire poem; and weeps again when he sees her, implacable in her wounded hatred, in the Underworld, having committed suicide out of grief.

In the second of the two odes addressed to his friend Virgil in Book 1, Horace takes issue with this extreme tearfulness. The poem starts with the death of the young Quintilius, much mourned by his friends, and none more than Virgil. Horace, in the gentlest way, is suggesting that there must be limits to weeping. Virgil's immoderate grief does not acknowledge the terms of the human condition; Quintilius, like other humans, was not entrusted to his friends for more than a single, limited life. He cannot be begged back.

But if this sounds harsh, Horace acknowledges that this acceptance is hard. Only patience makes it easier to bear what cannot be put right. Easier said than done.

What this little story of the friendship of Horace and Virgil shows is that friendship can and must involve disagreement. It is an active force, not a passive one. At its noblest and strongest it can resemble what we call therapy.

The deepest and most complicated friendship enacted in Horace's poetry is that with his patron Maecenas. Maecenas of course is not just any old friend, he is the man who has made his life's work possible, who has given him his spiritual home, the Sabine Farm. The first book of odes, the first book of satires, and the first book of epistles begin with poems addressed to Maecenas.

Maecenas, we gather from the later Roman writer Seneca, suffered from hypochondria. He was a man who had much on his shoulders. But he was also a complex, multifaceted character, himself a writer and poet, who cultivated the friendship of poets; that, of course, is what he is remembered for. The closest of these friendships was undoubtedly with Horace, whom on his death-bed he asked the emperor to "take care of, as if he were myself," who only survived him by fifty-nine days, and who was buried next to him on the Esquiline Hill. Perhaps Horace did not really want to outlive this man who had made his life's work possible, his constant, never-failing supporter, "the half of my soul."

What could Horace give back to this man who had given him everything? Obviously very little in the material sense. He could share a bottle of his own local wine, a modest bottle, not the kind of grand cru Maecenas would be served at official ban-quets. He could give his friendship.

Horace, much less grand than Maecenas by birth (Maecenas was descended from ancient kings), social position, and wealth, was also less hemmed in by the cares of state, the demands of official business, the whole immense task of running an empire. The Latin word *cura* means "care" and "anxiety." In one of his greatest and bleakest images Horace writes "behind the horseman's back sits Black Anxiety." No translation can fully catch the force of the Latin words "post equitem sedet atra cura": an "eques" is both a horseman, a knight, and a member of the equestrian order, the Roman aristocracy. And "atra cura," "black care," encompasses worry, anxiety, depression: a horrible, dark personification of the negative forces that feed on life and destroy the possibility of enjoyment. However hard the horseman spurs his horse, how-ever fast the horse gallops, he will never outrun the black care that sits behind him. The only way is to turn around and face it.

So at least I found, when a love crisis in my thirties brought me black terror, a dark cycle of anxiety and sleeplessness I could not break. I felt hounded. Something was on my track, call it black care or the black dog, and I could not shake it off.

It was time to go into therapy, to sit in a room with a stranger and let the "lion griefs," as W. H. Auden called them, emerge from the shade.

Years passed. I competed with my therapist (a New Yorker who I fantasized might have been Woody Allen's therapist, the one in *Hannah and Her Sisters* who "became so frustrated, he put in a salad bar"), tried to understand psychoanalysis, phenomenology, existentialism, Heidegger, Derrida, Levinas. But of course that was not really the point. This was not another intellectual puzzle to be mastered.

This was something else, a kind of relationship about relationship, a relationship in which patterns played out in previous relationships might be recognized. What would happen if the familiar pattern was not repeated, if the old record was not endlessly replayed?

I started to have dreams about fishermen, ship captains (I was on my own, in a lifeboat, surrounded by sharks), the Jewish first violinist of a string quartet playing in an upstairs room. Might these dream figures have anything to do with him, Leon gently asked? At first I was skeptical. Why should they have anything to do with him?

But over time there came an acknowledgment, an opening, a warming. I felt I had been something like a yeti, an abominable snowman, inhabiting a cold, inhospitable realm that needed to be traversed alone. The template for this realm was Farleigh House Preparatory School, where glasses of water froze overnight in the dormitories, where we froze watching rugby in shorts on winter afternoons ("Come on, Farleigh!" we bellowed, imitating the snuff-taking lover of Chaucer and Cervantes, Frank MacAdam). From that point on I had never trusted my feelings to anyone.

Much fear needed to be overcome. Surely no normal, warm-blooded human being would want to come into contact with an abominable snowman. Wouldn't he freeze the life out of whoever came too close?

But as the therapy proceeded, I experienced a general warming up, or thawing, of relationships, a lowering of defenses. Perhaps for the first time in my life I was able to enjoy a relatively open or unguarded friendship. Even more important, I was able to begin to learn what Horace left as one of his last lessons, in the conclusion of Epistles 1.18, "how to return you as a friend to yourself."

Both therapy and friendship are conducted through words—an obvious point perhaps, but not so obvious if you looked more closely. There are words and words. Therapy is a kind of litmus test or sifter of words, sorting out the chaff and the chatter—the words designed to keep the other person off the track, to numb or befuddle—from those which ring true, which sound out from the heart. And such words never exist in isolation. They are always answering words. It is when you hear the words that ring true, the words that show that someone else has answered to your experience, that you in turn can speak with what Lacan (in one of his more comprehensible moments) called "full" rather than "empty" speech.

In that sense, poetry, therapy, and friendship are all related. Is it anachronistic to suggest that Horace, the poet-friend of Maecenas, was offering his patron a kind of therapy? I don't think so, especially because of what Horace's philosophical mentor, Epicurus, had to say about suffering and the soul.

Maecenas undoubtedly suffered more than his share of "atra cura." Time and again Horace seems to be trying to lift the overburdened statesman's mood. Strangely, the son of a freed slave, the man who has given up the sword and the shield he left ingloriously behind on the battlefield of Philippi for the pen, who has done nothing more (or less) than write verses, can offer the worldly statesman a wisdom and a balm he will not find anywhere else.

I detect a double envy in this friendship. Maecenas surely envied his friend's talent as a poet; the fragment of Maecenas's verse that survives in Suetonius's *Life of Horace* is lame indeed.

The apparently humble freedman's son, Horace, is the one who will have the last laugh, raising a monument in the form of the Odes that will last longer than any of the grand architectural edifices of the empire. Not only that, but they will survive miraculously intact, even improving with age.

Horace perhaps envied Maecenas his splendid social position and beyond that his ability to deploy his talents in a field wider than the narrow furrow of poetry. Horace's friendship with Maecenas was undoubtedly complicated by the fact that Maecenas was also his patron; they were not equals, in obvious senses. But what are the Odes, if not an assertion of the power of the apparently small and modest in the face of overweening pride and grandeur?

TO MAECENAS (ODES 3.29)

You fret about the right course for our state—
How to frame the city's governance,
What further murderous mayhem's being planned
In Basra by Moqtada, and the Taliban.

The future outcome and the end of this
Look dark as midnight: that's God's gift to us;
Straining to know too much, too far ahead,
We blind and fool ourselves; what's present, now

Is what we can address in equanimity.
Everything else flows past us like a river,
Sometimes gliding by in perfect peace
Like some eternal movement toward the sea,

Sometimes in spate, rolling boulders down
Its bed, uprooting trees, and sweeping houses,

Cattle, people to their doom in a roar
That shakes the underpinnings of the earth.

Who is the truly happy human being,
Who can at least keep calmness in her soul?
Is it the one whose mind's one move ahead,
Or looking back with infinite regret?

I say this: happy is she or he
Who can tell you, "Today I've lived";
The storm may come tomorrow or the sun
At noon; there's nothing any power can do

To unweave that thread, erase the living trace—
No fate undoes the living that we've done,
Although we cannot hold the hour, the day,
Which flows and having flown will not return.

And as for Lady Luck, I like her visits
But don't expect she'll stick around for long.
I know she has her savage side and loves
To switch her favors, mixing kind and cruel.

In a whir of wings she'll whisk away success
And fame and fortune you thought firmly fixed.
Accepting loss I'll woo an honest girl
Called Poverty, and trust my inner voice.

Sometimes a life raft's better than a ship;
I'll row my little two-oared skiff to safety
Urged on by the breath of poetry,
Following the friendly guidance of the stars.

Nine

Town Mouse and Country Mouse

The first time I visited Rome everything seemed simpler, and certainly more exciting. I was eleven; it was the spring of 1969, just before the beginning of the Easter holidays, and my mother tried to extract me early from my prep school. That act of parental daring called forth a moralistic address to the entire school from the headmaster. If parents decided they could take their children out of school whenever it suited them, even for purportedly educational reasons, where would it all end?

I remember the plane journey, the first I had ever made; flying over the jagged, gleaming Alps for the very first time, seeing my father order a Campari, in true Roman style, as an *aperitivo*. On our arrival at the airport someone patted me on the head and called me "bambino." I didn't mind in the least; in fact, I responded to the warmth.

We stayed at a beautiful hotel just inside the northern edge of the pine-fringed ancient walls, near the Villa Borghese. Its evocative name was Hotel Eliseo. From the top terrace you could see the dome of St. Peter's—whose combination of heavenly thrust upward and gathering, nurturing roundness resonated with profound needs in my soul. Nearby there was a trattoria called Il Piccolo Mondo where we had antipasti, salami, octopus salad, mozzarella, artichoke hearts. This was the food, wonderfully new and attractive to me, the country that my mother loved;

at age eighteen she had done an exchange with an Italian girl, and they have remained friends ever since.

Perhaps the best thing of all was the breakfasts in bed, which we learned to order in Italian, *prima colazione per quattro persone*, which for once we ate all together, not separate in boarding schools, my sister and I coming through to join my parents from our room, which abutted theirs.

I've been back to Rome maybe half a dozen times since; as a lovesick student, hopelessly pursuing a green-eyed beauty whose father worked for the Food and Agriculture Organization of the UN; as a brooding young man, on the trail of Caravaggio, meeting two wonderful, witty Dutch sisters, laughing with them at some grand ambassadorial party when I grabbed a chair that was supporting a huge wardrobe, causing this immense piece of furniture to topple over; stopping over with my mother for a couple of days one blazing June en route to her old friend's younger daughter's wedding in Umbria.

I can't say I have got to know or understand Rome better in the intervening years. I find it a confusing place these days, difficult to get to the heart of.

Unconsciously on this return trip more than forty years after the first, I have chosen a hotel not far from the Eliseo, on the other side of the via Veneto. It is a magical Roman spring once again, Judas trees putting out flowers the deep color of raspberry sorbet, orange blossom–scented air.

One evening after a walk in the Borghese gardens, where a few couples are spreading late picnics, while others are speaking on mobile phones as they jog, I go to see whether I can find the old hotel.

I am somehow surprised to find that the Eliseo is still there, where it always was, I suppose, in the via di Porta Pinciana. I walk into the lobby and tell the concierge I stayed at this hotel as a boy. I'm not sure whether he believes me. The decoration in the lobby seems rather faded, and certainly dated, in a not very attractive 1960s style; the whole place is in need of refurbishment. Perhaps the sumptuousness of the hotel in my imagination is a trick of memory. I walk out rather abruptly, not giving myself the chance to see St. Peter's dome one more time from the roof terrace.

It is dinnertime and I think about eating at Il Piccolo Mondo, but the restaurant has changed beyond recognition, and seems smart and characterless instead of what I remember as inviting and unpretentious, and I choose instead a place called Osteria Localino, which cannot summon any memories. The only other couple eating there are also English, and we get into a strange conversation about the chain of eateries started up in England by an Italian in the 1960s called Berni Inns.

Horace complained about "fumum, opes, strepitumque Romae"; the pollution, the ostentatious wealth, the noise. Perhaps he also found Rome fascinating and baffling, attractive and maddening at the same time. It was at least, in his day, the undisputed center of power. Now it seems to me a city of ruins, museums, and churches, a collection of monuments without connection; I don't get the thread of Rome.

After a few days in the city I start to feel slightly crazy. I have set myself a punishing schedule of sightseeing, avoiding the most obvious sights. I have not gone so far as a Spanish artist friend who based his residency at the Spanish Academy on the premise that he must not at any point catch sight of the Colosseum. I think the terrible tension, the fear that at any moment one could be caught out by a careless glimpse of the monumental slaughterhouse, would have been too much for me.

Manuel had to go to extraordinary lengths to avoid the place, though he did allow himself to be brought there blindfolded so that he could touch and even smell the stone. There were no traces of blood apparently.

One quite distant sighting of the Colosseum is enough for me. Even Colosseo metro is best avoided; the trains, reasonably bearable on either side of the stop, become intolerably crowded as you approach the station, as if the tourists have some unconscious wish to emulate the experience of the doomed gladiators.

Thank God Horace died a century before the Flavian amphitheater was constructed—though not, as one can deduce from his poems, before gladiatorial combat became a popular sport. I hope, I very much hope, that Horace would have shared the good taste of his successor and admirer Seneca in trying to steer clear of the place. Surely its vulgar monumentality and excessiveness would have appalled him.

There are so many tourists at all the main Roman sites or sights that one cannot really see the sights, but rather see only the tourists seeing or not seeing the sights. One has to be caught unaware by them, so that my glimpse of the Baths of Caracalla when I came into Rome on the airport bus on the first evening is more telling than an earnest attempt to view the Roman Forum. I should have recalled what another visitor to Rome, the Spanish Baroque poet Francisco de Quevedo, said nearly four hundred years before me: "You're seeking Rome in Rome, pilgrim / And in Rome itself you won't find Rome; / Its walls are nothing but a corpse / And the Aventine its own tomb."

Just for a moment I see the baths as I imagine other visitors down the ages must have seen them: gigantic, preternaturally large, dwarfing all other constructions until our own age.

Setting out on foot from my hotel the next morning, I walk first down the via Veneto, once the center of smart Rome but now nothing but a boring, empty succession of five-star hotels. Everywhere there are references to Fellini, playing on the false idea of *La Dolce Vita* as something gloriously hedonistic, ignoring the fact that he intended his great film as an excoriating exposé of the terrible emptiness at the heart of hedonism, its blindness to love. So Rome mistakes its own.

I am heading for a relatively obscure museum, the part of the Museo Nazionale housed in the Palazzo Altemps. It is one of the most important collections of antique art housed in Rome, and thus in the world, but because it is not as famous as the Vatican or Capitoline collections, it attracts very few tourists. I should be looking at the Roman things, I suppose, but though I do notice a fine head of Zeus, a bust of Antinous, a Hermes, there is one piece of sculpture in the museum that stands out from all the others: the exquisite and haunting Ludovisi throne, a Greek sculpture from around 450 B.C., perhaps from the Greek colony of Locri Epizefiri in Calabria, part of what came to be called Magna Graecia.

It consists of an oblong block of marble, like a small altar. On the front a beautiful woman whose breasts show through her thin tunic is being pulled up—perhaps pulled out of the sea—by two attendants. On the left side panel a naked flute-girl sits cross-legged, playing a double flute. The right side panel shows a hooded woman placing incense in a burner.

Everything about this object is exquisitely graceful, delicate, unmannered. In a single gentle breath it blows away all the coarse monumental, derivative, empty statuary with which Rome is still filled; it inhabits a different air, in contact with the muses. In the same room as the Ludovisi Throne is the Ludovisi Acrolith, the head of a goddess smiling the famous archaic smile.

The air breathed by the Ludovisi throne is the air that entranced Horace. It is the air, transported to Italy, breathed by the Greek lyric poets who inspired him, whose delicate, graceful, forceful music he wanted to bring—for the first time—to Latin verse. He would have seen sculptures like this in Athens, adorning the Parthenon; not just the famous friezes but Phidias's chryselephantine statue of Athene, one of the wonders of the ancient world, and so many other marvels still intact.

It is not at all un-Horatian to feel the Ludovisi throne is ineffably graceful and superior compared to the coarse productions of the Romans; quite the reverse. Horace, whom we think of as a quintessential Roman, was in many ways an anti-Roman.

Very few of the monuments we think of as stereotypically Roman have anything to do with Horace. The Colosseum, the triumphal arches of Titus and Constantine, the columns of Trajan and Antoninus and Marcus Aurelius, the baths of Diocletian and Caracalla: these are all productions of the later empire, contradictions of Horace's minimalist ethos, profoundly un-Horatian.

You might make an exception for the Pantheon, not far from the Palazzo Altemps, the next stop on my sightseeing itinerary, the greatest of all Roman buildings, whose noble Corinthian portico carries an inscription saying "Marcus Agrippa, son of Lucius, having been consul three times, built it"—Marcus Agrippa the great general of Augustus and beautifier of Rome, who was a contemporary of Horace.

The majestic domed structure is imposing without being overwhelming, impressing with its perfect proportions rather than its sheer size. But like everything else in Rome it is a palimpsest, written and rewritten; it turns out that very little remains of the original building constructed by Agrippa. The structure you can see, with its amazing coffered ceiling, dates from the time of Hadrian, but this in turn has been rewritten and reinterpreted by the Catholic Church, which, speaking through insistent signs, tells you that "this is a religious building. We ask you to remain silent." The Pantheon, apparently, has become the basilica of Santa Maria ad Martyres, colloquially known as Santa Maria Rotonda. A rather cold statue called the *Madonna del Sasso*, made by Lorenzetti, looks down over the tomb of Raphael. The tourists take no notice.

Wandering somewhat aimlessly, I suddenly fall into a real bit of Rome, the via del Governo Vecchio, a street of restaurants patronized by Romans. In the Pizzeria Mimi e Coco, drinking a cold beer, I watch a group of three young Romans sipping Camparis, an older man eating on his own, in a polo shirt and corduroy jacket, with a white dog with brown ears, like a hunting dog in a fresco.

My moment of feeling at home does not last. The city is beginning to grate on my nerves and I need to get out. I want to follow Horace's own route, as far as possible; that is, to head out toward his own beloved farm in the Sabine hills, twenty kilometers or so beyond Tivoli, the ancient Roman town of Tibur, where Horace ~~also may have~~ owned a property.

I have researched "Horace's villa" in the modern way; that is, using the Internet, or more specifically Google, and the results seem promising. There is even a website called the Horace's Villa Project devoted to an archaeological dig done between 1997 and 2001 at a site near the small hill town of Licenza. The dig was a serious affair, conducted under "the institutional sponsorship of the American Academy in Rome, UCLA, and the Archaeological Superintendency for Lazio of the Italian Ministry of Culture."

You can even visit the site online, as I discover weeks after my return to London, when I get around to writing up my notes. I am very glad I did not discover this before I set off on my pilgrimage, even though the virtual guided tour by the well-coiffed and luxuriantly mustachioed professor Bernard Frischer, the director of the dig, is rather good, cheerful and informative. The thing is, it is almost too good; it might have discouraged me from going there in the first place.

Professor Frischer is not the first archaeologist or antiquary to gravitate to the Licenza site as the possible location of Horace's Sabine Farm. The German Catholic humanist, and later Vatican librarian, Lucas Holstenius in the seventeenth century identified the Licenza river as Horace's Digentia and Horace's "ruined temple of Vacuna" as a site near the neighboring village of Roccagiovine. In the next century a bitter quarrel broke out between the two abbots Domenico de Sanctis and Capmartin de Chaupy about who was the first to find the exact site. You might well ask why two clerics should have become so exercised over Horace, that sparing and infrequent worshipper of the gods.

The first excavations were undertaken in 1760–61 by the

Baron de Saint Odile, a Frenchman from Lorraine who became Tuscan ambassador to Rome and lived in style in the Villa Medici. In the following decades the place became popular with artists; Allan Ramsay viewed the mosaics in 1775 and the German artist Philipp Augustus Hackert painted a series of gouaches, now in the Goethe museum in Düsseldorf. They convey a rather charming sense of late-eighteenth-century bourgeois life rather than anything to do with Horace.

Then a major excavation, including extensive rebuilding, which did much to create the site as we see it, was carried out between 1911 and 1914 by the Italian archaeologist Angelo Pasqui. This excavation was interrupted first by the war and then by the unexpected death of Pasqui in 1915.

What Frischer does not stress in the online tour, but does make clear in his big scholarly book about his excavation, is that "the original objective, proving whether or not this was the villa of Horace, was not able to be answered." No tile or lead pipe engraved or stamped with the poet's name has been found. Perhaps that would not have been his style, though it was quite common for Romans to stamp their tiles and pipes. Even so, the site at Licenza fits with all the references, however tantalizingly oblique, in Horace's poetry; surely it is worth a visit.

Getting to Licenza, about fifty kilometers from Rome, is not as easy as you might think. The nearest train station is at Mandela, ten kilometers away; the Horace's villa project website helpfully informs you that there are no taxis at this station. I spend an hour or two investigating buses on the impenetrable Cotral bus website, which probably displays every bus route in the province of Lazio but not in a manner that can be decoded by a foreigner.

There seems no alternative but to hire a car, something I am loath to do in Rome, which has some of the worst signage and the most dangerous drivers in the Western world. Once before I was nearly killed by a mad Roman driver, as I stood on the pavement somewhere near St. Peter's in the early hours of New Year's Day 1982. It turns out that I will only just escape with my life this time, like Horace from his falling tree, but that is many hours into the future.

I wake up early on a beautiful sunny Roman spring morning to walk down from my hotel on via Sicilia to the car hire office in the bowels of Stazione Termini. The fatherly middle-aged man in the office detects my nervousness immediately—how I wish I could keep it better hidden—and guides me through the procedures with kindly patience.

Of course getting out of Rome is not remotely easy; I manage to miss the sign to the Grande Raccordo Anulare ring road and find myself in an area of anonymous-looking suburban avenues with no signage. Just avoiding panic, I execute an illegal U-turn (but what is that in Rome?) and manage to retrace my way to the ring-road entrance. Suddenly I am on the A24 motorway heading toward L'Aquila, and hardly take in the way the gentle hills around Tivoli bathed in spring sunshine turn into what in the British Isles would be called mountains; the steep, rocky ranges of the Monti Lucretili densely covered in a rich variety of trees and shrubs, with stony hill towns perched on inaccessible-looking peaks. I wasn't expecting scenery as grand as this, more Wordsworth's Lake District than Pope's "Epistle to Burlington."

Licenza, one of the hill towns, is only a few kilometers from the motorway turn-off; following the via Licinese, I drive along the valley of Horace's Digentia, the cool stream he liked to bathe in; even though outdoor bathing in rivers and lakes is an enthusiasm I share with Horace, there doesn't seem enough water for a proper dip and I haven't brought my trunks.

Shortly before Licenza, on the right-hand side of the road, a large brown sign indicates a left turn for the archaeological site. Allowing no room for doubt, it states "the poet Quintus Horatius Flaccus (65–8 B.C.) lived in this place."

The ruins are a short, steep drive up a cobbled road. The site is a kind of saddle ("on the ridge of a steep wood," as the Town Mouse says in Satires 2.6, so that fits) looking toward Licenza and the high hills beyond on one side and into other hills heading back toward Tivoli and Rome on the other.

Getting out of the car, I take a deep breath, of relief and gratitude, at having survived at least one leg of the journey. And my first impression is that you could not wish to find a place of more idyllic, tranquil beauty. If it is not Horace's farm, it should be.

There is no museum, no tourist shop, no turnstile. I am the only visitor on this Saturday morning. No sound in the air but the liquid chatter of warblers. After a while, a sweet-looking man in his late sixties appears, the custodian, Alfredo.

Our conversation is hampered by my poor Italian but I understand him when he points me in the direction of the "fons Bandusiae." This turns out to be an elaborate Renaissance water feature called the Ninfeo degli Orsini, which almost certainly has nothing to do with the humble natural spring Horace celebrated in what for me is the most beautiful of the Odes.

The remains of the villa seem substantial, but not grand (though archaeologists reckon that the residence in its first-century A.D. incarnation covered twenty thousand square feet, which is about twenty times the size of my small house in London); there are the brick walls of the various rooms of the villa, leading off a central atrium, rising about two feet from the ground; and considerably taller and more impressive, in the far corner of the site, near the custodian's house, a bath complex. For those who want to preserve the image of a modest Horace and an unpretentious villa, there is no need to despair; this grand bath complex is a later development, from the first century A.D.

Above all, the place feels green and bucolic. Where once there was a porticoed garden, ninety yards long, with a large pool, now tall firs, cypresses, and ash trees create the effect of a shaded park. Everywhere there are wildflowers, cyclamen, daisies, wild geranium.

Of course the naive and sentimental view of the pilgrim that he or she is walking in Horace's footsteps here needs to be corrected by a bracing dose of Horatian skepticism. Even if this was Horace's farm, the site is largely a reconstruction, representing Pasqui's idea of what a site should look like. Very little that one can see dates from the first century B.C.; nearly everything, as Frischer's excavations have made clear, is at least a century later.

And yet there is something immemorially benign in the beauty of the place, and there is at least a chance, perhaps a good chance, that this was the beloved ground the poet walked on, the piece of earth he called "the fulfilment of all my prayers."

I am raised from reverie by Alfredo, coming to tell me that I should visit the museum in Licenza, housing the finds from the site, before it closes at noon.

Licenza, a couple of kilometers away, is a typical medieval Italian hill town, small and unpretentious, gray stone streets winding up in snail fashion to the beetling Orsini castle. Here the air could hardly be more different; it is feudal and Catholic, not Horatian and polytheistic; dark and brooding, not green and bucolic.

At the very top of the tiny town there is an irregular square surrounded by the various bits of the baronial castle. I knock on the door marked "Museo" and am answered by the volunteer custodian, a slightly cross-eyed middle-aged woman. Once again I am the only visitor; the custodian, perhaps a little bored and wanting someone to talk to, shows me around with fanatical zeal. She tells me that this was the former wine and oil storeroom of the castle, the coldest part of the building; and though the sun is blazing outside, the museum has a tomblike chill.

My cross-eyed guide is not content to allow me to browse through the miscellany of bits of fresco, marble decoration, lead

piping; she wants me to see everything. But above all she wants
me to appreciate how richly decorated and beautiful the place
was in its heyday; "it was a dream," "era un sogno," she keeps
repeating. And she has a point; the marble ceiling boss of acanthus, a delicate marble ornament with frogs' feet, the still brightly
colored fragments of fresco, all speak of the utmost refinement of
taste. If Horace's villa was decorated like this, it was stretching at
the limits of his phrase "simplex munditiis," artfully simple.

My guide seems rather disappointed when, having examined
every last fragment of fresco and section of pipe, I say I must
leave; she thrusts the program for a Horace conference that took
place the previous summer into my hand as a parting gift.

I can only take so much immersion in the past. I need coffee,
and then something to eat. The Orazio Garden Bar—Horace's
joint—in the main square at the bottom of the town is the obvious spot. Everything here is rough and ready, warm and human;
a grandfather leads his grandson around the fountain on a toy
tractor. I suddenly feel a sense of disconnection; despite the insincere tribute paid by the names, Orazio Garden Bar, via Orazio,
this unsophisticated Italian village life, revolving around children,
surely has nothing to do with the bachelor poet who lived in such
refinement twenty centuries ago, surrounded by frescoes, mosaics, marble, and fishponds, immersed in his reading of Greek
poets and philosophers. What would these down-to-earth types
make of the perfumed, togaed, sexually ambivalent maker of odes,
shunner of vulgar crowds, and what would he make of them? No
wonder that there is remarkably little effort made in Licenza to
cash in on "the Horace phenomenon."

I notice that the square I am sitting in is called Piazza della
Libertà. I suppose this refers to the Risorgimento, the liberation
of Italy from foreign and papal domination in the nineteenth
century, but Horace might have been amused by the name, with
its fervent, grandiose ring. How easy is it to achieve liberation,
for a person, for a country? For what did Horace's father buy his

freedom? So that he could give his brilliant son the best education money could buy, which then liberated him, Horace—to become a poet.

I buy some bread, mortadella, and tomatoes from the friendly village store just off the piazza and go to eat my picnic next to the monument to Horace on the edge of the town, looking back toward the farm in the hills. As usual, the monument is an idealized, generalized vision of the exalted bard, a marble travesty of the living poet. But at least the spot and the view are beautiful, new leaves delicately hazing all the hillsides, a strong sun and a warm breeze coming up from the south.

I open my battered red Loeb edition of the Odes at the seventeenth ode of Book 1, in which Horace speaks of this landscape and its particular, saving music.

THESE ITALIAN HILLS (ODES 1.17)

You make quick changes, furry Faunus,
God of woods and fields, quit Arcady
And come to these Italian hills,
Keep my herds safe from rain and roasting.

Thanks to you my she-goats roam
unharmed, the wives of Stinking Billy,
Root out the hidden herbs and shrubs;
The kids need not fear glass-green vipers

Or warlike wolves; so long, my sweet,
As all the sounding valleys hereabouts,
The smooth-stoned riverbeds ring out
With music from your rustic flute.

The gods (you see) protect me; while
I live and write in simple truth,

The horn of country fruits and flowers
Will brim for you, my dearest one.

No one will harm you here, in my
Creative hideaway you'll sing
Of Ulysses, the temptress Circe
And his wife Penelope.

And you can drink—the summer wine
Won't make sore heads or hangovers
Or lead us into arguments,
About your ex, that utterly

Uncouth young bruiser, quite unsuited
To you, Tyndaris dear, the one
Who ripped your headdress off
And practically raped you.

Connection is restored. The deep, heartfelt beauty of the ode and the loveliness of the landscape echo each other.

At its heart the poem speaks of protection, of keeping safe from violence. The key words that ring through it in Latin are "defendit" (defend, ward off), "impune" (safely), "tuentur" (protect, keep safe). The god of the countryside, whom the Romans called Faunus and Greeks called Pan, will protect not just Horace's livestock but him and his love, who may not be any more real, in a literal sense, than the nymphs in Mallarmé's "L'Après-midi d'un faune."

The love may be idealized but the attacks, from deadly snakes and wolves and rough sexual assault, seem quite real. Key to this protection is music, the Muse, poetry; the pipe music of Greek Pan transmuted into Latin verses; native "woodnotes wild" imbued with farther-off echoes.

Poetry, Horace's mastery of meters, his amazing feat in being the first to adapt Greek lyric song to Latin measures, is what has brought him protection, not least in the form of the Sabine Farm.

But though it conveys a profound sense of happiness, this poem is not selfish or gloating; the protection really comes from the gods, to whom Horace and his music are dear and endearing, and they are dear because of their "piety," their quiet devotion to peace, their turning away from rapine and violence.

It is time to go back to the farm for a little more wandering and communing with the spirit of the poet who may or may not have lived there two thousand years ago, but whose benign influence has kept it safe, from—for example—developers, mining companies, crazed road builders, an excess of tourists. This safekeeping, in an era of mass destruction, is almost miraculous, on a par with the survival, the safekeeping, of Horace's poetry.

This time I am not alone. A man and a woman in their seventies, dressed for hiking, definitely not Italian, possibly Canadian, too quiet to be American, are inspecting the ruins, and I go up to them and ask what has brought them to this spot. Colin Anderson is a modern languages professor from the South Island of New Zealand who has made a retirement study of Horace. He has published a translation of the first book of odes, under the title *Harvesting the Day*, using the original meters. With great generosity he gives me a copy to take home. Later I will read some of the translations and admire the metrical ingenuity while concluding that the attempt to reproduce Horace's meters exactly in English, while valuable in some ways, is unlikely to yield translations that live as contemporary poems.

There is something impressive about these serious, friendly people, not young and not in the best of health—Colin's wife in particular seems quite frail and shaky—and the immense distance they have traveled to make their Horatian pilgrimage. They have also taken in Horace's hometown of Venosa and Monte Soratte (Horace's Soracte) a little west of here. Horace, who predicted with no false modesty that his verses would reach the farthest corners of the known world, would not have been surprised, but I think he would have been touched.

After they have retreated to a far recess of the site to eat their picnic, I lie down for a while on a flat piece of stone, soaking up the sun and the birdsong, clearing my mind of thought. I drift off. A light touch on my trouser leg jolts me awake; it is a small green lizard, fortunately not a glass-green viper, which has mistaken me for part of the ruins. Perhaps it would not be such a bad fate to become part of the ruins here.

Maybe I have ducked the big question raised by the Licenza excavations; if this is Horace's farm, even though we may never establish the exact floorplan of the original villa, he lived in considerable style and luxury even, in a big or at least biggish house, with far more than the "little corner" of land he refers to.

One answer, I think, is provided for me on the way back to Rome. Driving past Tivoli, inundated in tourist buses and impossible to park in, I decide on the spur of the moment to stop off at Hadrian's villa a few kilometers outside the modern town.

I had some idea of the Villa Adriana as one of Italy's grandest Roman sites, but nothing has prepared me for its immensity. The scale is breathtaking; no one in the world today, not Silvio Berlusconi at his most vulgar, not the richest men in the world, Bill Gates (studiedly modest of course) or Carlos Slim, has a villa like this, the size of a town, the size, almost, of Pompeii. Surrounded by olive groves, with the Monti Lucretili rising behind, the place is also majestically beautiful. Hadrian, a man of taste, in love with Greek art and architecture, himself a poet, decorated it with the utmost refinement. Pert-buttocked male statues surround a pool the length of a short runway, reminding you of Hadrian's love for the exquisite Antinous, the Bithynian youth who drowned himself in the Nile in A.D. 130.

Compared to this opulent megavilla, Horace's farm could indeed be called modest. Scale and opulence are to some extent relative, and judged by the scale of the residences of seriously rich Romans such as Maecenas, Horace's villa—if it was Horace's villa, if it covered anything like the extent of the ruins we can see—was hardly extravagant.

The second answer or reflection is this. It is not really possible to go back to Horace's villa, in a literal sense, any more than it was possible for me to return to the Hotel Eliseo of my childhood. Horace's farm, over the centuries, has been transformed into a poetic symbol.

The idea of a way of living close to nature, sustained by a careful and devoted local husbandry, the cultivation of fruit trees, of vines and olives, the tending of livestock, allowed to roam freely, all of which provide the basis for a generous hospitality—this is one of the most potent ideas in our culture.

Horace to some extent created that idea, and he also knew that it would be more potent the more it was essentially modest and inclusive. The way of living represented by Hadrian's immense villa may be overwhelming in its grandeur, and impressive in its exquisite refinement, but in the end it is less powerful and inspiring than Horace's idea of the good life in the country. More is less.

This idea of the good life in the country has inspired innumerable poems, novels, works of nonfiction, TV series; it has also inspired countless individuals, many of whom may not know that their dream is Horatian.

The seminal poem in English inspired by this Horatian ideal is Ben Jonson's "To Penshurst," which begins like this:

Thou art not, Penshurst, built to envious show
    Of touch or marble, nor canst boast a row
Of polished pillars, or a roof of gold;
    Thou hast no lantern whereof tales are told,
Or stairs, or courts; but stand'st an ancient pile,
    And these grudged at, art reverenced the while.
Thou joy'st in better marks, of soil, of air,
    Of wood, of water; therein thou art fair.

Once again it does not matter how big the actual Penshurst was, and is: the point is that it projects an image of order, natural, agricultural, social, environmental, ethical. The house sits naturally, not grandly, in its own Kentish landscape, built of the local stone, surrounded by woods and fields that are not just productive but haunted by poetry (this was the house of the great Sir Philip Sidney) and divinity.

The house does not beetle over the surrounding landscape, belittling its neighbors, but rather welcomes them, whoever they are: "all come in, the farmer and the clown." Penshurst is equally capable of entertaining the king and his son, out on a hunting expedition, and the "ripe daughters" of local country people. It has been built "with no man's ruin, no man's groan" and as a result does not provoke envy. Jonson knew all about envy just as Horace did: both rose from humble origins to be admired by aristocrats.

All wishful thinking? Of course. So the later poet W. B. Yeats ruefully concluded when he established himself in his own country house, the ancient Norman keep of Ballylee. For all his love of country houses and the elegant women who lived in them, he recognized that in some sense they were the result of, or an atonement for, violence.

Sitting now in the café at the entrance to the Villa Adriana, I reflect on the way Horace's idea, filtered through centuries and from the center of the Roman Empire to one of its farther-flung outposts, influenced my upbringing. I think my parents were motivated by a Horatian dream when in the 1950s they came to buy a house in the rolling Chiltern Hills, about the same distance from London as Horace's farm is from the walls of Rome. This was the house where I grew up—the house with its two-acre garden that seemed immense, the big old trees, the small orchard, the vegetable patch.

Rising behind the house is the village common; land once

communally used for grazing, now overgrown with wild cherry and hawthorn; in front of the house fields billow toward a beech wood.

The house is not too big and not too small. With its decorative, un-English shutters it has the look of a French villa. Closeness to nature was always part of its charm; in summer martins used to come and nest under the eaves (for some reason they don't anymore); you can still hear cuckoos, two or three species of warbler. The greenfinches, bullfinches, and yellowhammers that used to be abundant are less so, but the indomitable chaffinches remain. Now, in a kind of exchange, red kites wheel silently over the garden, twisting their great forked tails; higher up buzzards circle. Raptors in exchange for innocent grain eaters.

Sometimes nature comes altogether too close: *Glis glis* dormice regularly invade the wine cellar. Once I heard a rumble in the early morning and went downstairs to find that a retaining wall had collapsed, allowing water to pour off the common and flood the kitchen.

Heavy snowfalls can cut off the house and the village for days, and bring fears that big branches from the cedar will break and fall—they will not bear the weight.

Because I grew up here, it has given me my sense of the dear particularity of place, the rhythms of the seasons, the abundance and fecundity of nature. When I was a young boy, a man called (with wonderful aptness) Mr. Appleby used to tend the vegetable garden and orchard, which he himself had planted. He was already in his seventies and did not need to go on gardening, but he was hale and hearty and he loved it. I loved spending time with him, watching him dig the beds, unearth mysterious white potatoes and the orange spears of young carrots with their lacy frondage, which I would take down to the kitchen, where Ethel held court. Ethel, a tiny gray-haired Yorkshirewoman, had been my mother's stepmother's cook, had left in protest at the cruel treatment meted out to my mother, and then had come back soon after I was born, in effect to look after us all. She was much more like a grandmother to me than our cook.

While Mr. Appleby talked to me, a robin would perch on the handle of his spade, its breast the same color as the carrots, on the lookout for worms.

Ethel was the goddess of the store cupboard and of the kitchen, the living equivalent of the household gods, the Lares and Penates that Horace celebrated; warm smells of baking and roasting came up from the kitchen and drew my sister and me to watch her at work. We gazed in fascination as she kneaded dough, spread flour on the table, rolled the pastry with her rolling pin. She teased us with sly Yorkshire sayings when we pleaded for tidbits. I was pampered like a prince. Ethel, who had no children, gave us her no-nonsense love, laced with wit and irony as her cakes were laced with sherry. I sat with her in her warm miniature sitting room just off the kitchen as a soporific but reassuring voice intoned the soccer results, and Ethel kept her ears pricked for a score draw and a possible win in the pools.

My parents still live in the house, at the time of writing, though we all wonder how much longer they will be able to manage it, and I flinch away from the intolerable thought of their leaving it, of their leaving, of the house being left.

They still look after the big garden, with help, my mother watering the thirsty hydrangeas, though my father has finally given up mowing the steep lawns of the old chalk pit with his rotary mower. But he still serves chilled Mosel Kabinett on the lawn in front of the house, shaded by the tall cedar and the big spreading copper beech.

For decades now I have lived in London, with only occasional sorties to the country. London is where much of my work is, where most of my friends live, where I have made my life. I have adapted to London; I often feel happy to live in this city, which has so much to offer. I give thanks for its magnificent free museums, the National Gallery, where I can go for half an hour just to look at a favorite picture, the two contrasting Tates, the hidden splendors of the Wallace Collection. I belong to a tennis club, in a beautiful outdoor setting, which provides blessed relief from being cooped up in the study, and to the London Library, a haven right in the center of the city, with its air of nineteenth-century humanism.

But if asked where my soul was, I would always say it was in the country, because the mysteries of nature, of the sighing wind in the branches of the beeches, the cry of the owls at night, the sudden crisp confectionery of snow, seem so much deeper than the urgently artificial rhythms of the city. Apparently when I was a very young boy, taken up to the city by my parents to consult a doctor about my eczema, I announced very earnestly, "Don't like London, don't like the noise."

Is there a possibility of reconciliation? We have made a small garden, the size of an average room, but full of assorted plants, shrubs, a small prunus, a dwarf apple tree, myrtle, viburnum, euphorbia, bamboo, and ceanothus. We have no idea about gardening, but we love our small garden, and feel immeasurably proud when birds are drawn to nest in it. One year we had robins, blue tits, and blackbirds raising their young in succession, and we felt almost like parents ourselves as we watched the naive fledglings hopping around our small garden table and two chairs, horribly vulnerable to cats and sparrow hawks.

Our garden, as well as London's panoply of parks both big and small, makes me think of the saving Roman idea of *rus in urbe*—the countryside in the city. That is a post-Horatian idea, coined by the poet Martial nearly a hundred years after Horace wrote his odes.

Horace in fact, in the end, opted pretty firmly for the country. In his most revealing collection, the first book of epistles, you get the impression of a man and poet in some ways troubled and restless, yet also pretty firmly settled in the Sabine Farm.

Take the tenth epistle, in which he writes, as "a lover of the country" to his friend the city boy Aristius Fuscus: "You're mad about your city pad: I praise the lilting streams, the moss which grows on rocks, the echoing woods."

But he could admit to pulls in both directions. The most famous expression of this is the fable of the Town and Country Mouse from the second book of satires, one of the most charming and delightful things Horace ever penned.

The Country Mouse is entertaining his friend the Town Mouse in his rustic retreat—which is, in part, an allegory of Horace entertaining Maecenas in the Sabine Farm. The fare is simple and homely, a mix of grains spiced up with the odd raisin and bit of bacon, reserved for the guest. Eventually the Town Mouse has had enough (and I can quite understand his feelings about spelt). "Aren't people and the city superior to wild woods? And don't you know your days are numbered, and isn't it better to enjoy the good life?"

The Country Mouse is persuaded; in a trice they have crept under the city walls and find themselves feasting on leftovers from a plutocrat's banquet. Roles are reversed: the Town Mouse acts as waiter, with the Country Mouse stretched out on cloths of purple, sampling a succession of exquisite dishes. So far, so good; but then comes a terrible clanging of doors and the barking of ferocious hounds. You can see the fable as a gentle satire on the way the city stirs up desire. But only someone who had experienced the pull of both city and country could have written it.

Actually I think there must have been times when Horace thoroughly enjoyed being in Rome. He clearly relished wandering on his own among the markets, asking about the price of greens and flour, thinking his own thoughts; he enjoyed what he called "the cheating Circus"; he even rather enjoyed being pointed at, as a kind of celebrity, the minstrel of the Roman lyre, halfway between Bob Dylan and Seamus Heaney.

Where I think Horace can help us most of all is not in leading us to some rural idyll where we can definitively put the city
behind us, but in acknowledging the pull in both directions.
Horace once again claims that wonderful poetic privilege of being inconsistent, which is to say being human.

For all his professed belief, which was quite sincere, in the
superiority of the country, he continued to shuttle to and fro, to
be a town mouse and a country mouse. As his slave Davus reminds him, on the day when slaves are allowed to speak their
mind, "Horace, you're a fickle creature; when in Rome, you pine
for the country, but when you're in the country you praise Rome."
Yes, there are times when Rome, or London, or New York, is utterly maddening, when the noise and the pollution and the little
dogs in their tailor-made waistcoats and boots drive you crazy,
but there are other times when the city is the only place to be.

It's time for me to head back to Rome; I have promises to
keep, more sights to see.

On the way back in the late afternoon from the Villa Adriana
I decide to take not the motorway but the old slow road, the via
Tiburtina, whose pace suits my mood. Getting close to Rome,
the road becomes lined with warehouses selling cheap garden
ornaments, garages, petrol stations, but everything is bathed in
the serene light of Roman spring. I seem to be gliding back,
without the alarms of the journey out. It's too good to be true;
within sight of the walls, as I drive slowly along a wide avenue, a
car shoots across my bows, coming from where I can't imagine,
doing at least seventy miles per hour. I slam on the brakes; the
car just misses me, or so I think until I get out of it and see a
scratch along the front bumper. It was as close as that.

If the car hadn't missed me, I suppose I might have ended up
either in the Underworld, listening to Sappho singing (as Horace
imagines when he escapes the falling tree), or even to Horace
himself, or in the place that is next on my list. This is a cemetery

for poets (and others) that looks over the Aurelian Wall to one of the oddest ancient monuments in Rome, and one of our closest visual links to Horace's time.

The marble burial pyramid of the magistrate Caius Cestius, who died four years before Horace in 12 B.C., is everything Horace's Odes are not—grandiose, pretentious, self-serving, empty. It has preserved the name of Caius Cestius, but for what?

Thomas Hardy, visiting the nearby Protestant Cemetery in 1887, was moved to write his poem "Rome at the Pyramid of Cestius Near the Graves of Shelley and Keats," which includes these withering lines, "Who, then, was Cestius, / And what is he to me?" Cestius might have pointed indignantly to the inscription on his pyramid-tomb, which reads, "Caius Cestius, son of Lucius, of the gens Pobilia, member of the College of Epulones, praetor, tribune of the Plebs, septemvir of the Epulones."

In his own time he was a big cheese, a somebody. But in the longer span envisaged by Horace the big cheese has crumbled to nothing. Cestius's pyramid is an impressive thirty-seven meters high. But Horace, as he wrote in the triumphal conclusion to Odes 1–3, had completed a monument "higher than the pyramids."

Like Hardy (who possessed a well-thumbed and annotated collection of four books of poems by Horace), I have come to pay my respects not to Cestius but to Keats and Shelley, two English poets who died young in Italy in the 1820s and were buried in what became known as the Non-Catholic, or Protestant Cemetery.

They lie here together with hundreds of other artistic and nonartistic types, atheists, Jews, Muslims, the communist Antonio Gramsci, an Iranian ex–secret service officer gunned down by order of Ayatollah Khomeini, all overtaken by death in the Eternal City, and gravitating to this obscure, far corner of the city, part of the "meadows of the Roman people," just outside the city walls.

The spot had to be outside the city walls, because under papal law only Catholics could be buried within them. For centuries this wall must have seemed bizarre and gigantesque, enclosing hundreds of acres of fields and meadows. It took nearly fifteen hundred years from the fall of the Western Roman Empire for the city's population to reach the million or so the city contained in the time of Augustus.

When some of the better-off non-Catholic residents of Rome started to be buried here in the late eighteenth century, the place was still more *rus* than *urbs*, grazed by sheep and cattle when not used by people for recreation.

Traces of this Arcadian character survive, especially in the old part, shaded by two-hundred-year-old pines and cypresses. There are daisies and violets peeping through the grass on the spring day I come to pay my respects, as well as a tribe of preternaturally fat cats (no doubt fed by kindhearted English ladies), but no sheep or cattle. They would eat the daisies and violets, I suppose, like the pigs in Saki's "The Storyteller," that tale about a little girl who won medals for goodness and obedience that proved to be her undoing.

Keats was terribly ill all the time he spent in Rome, and sensed he had little time to live. On November 30, 1820, he wrote from Rome to his friend Charles Brown: "I have an habitual feeling of my real life having past, and that I am leading a posthumous existence." But this letter summons extraordinary resources of courage and affection; beyond those, of goodness. It is one of the most unbearable and magnificent letters you could ever read. What Keats himself finds unbearable is this thought: "I have been well, healthy, alert &c, walking with her—and now—the knowledge of contrast, feeling for light and shade, all that information necessary for a poem are great enemies to the recovery of the stomach." Even here Keats pulls back from despair, in surprisingly Horatian spirit: "You must bring your philosophy to bear—as I do mine, really—or how should I be able to live?"

Less than four months after he wrote that letter, Keats was on his deathbed, in the narrow room with a tall ceiling that you can visit in the Keats-Shelley House, looking over the Spanish Steps. His friend the painter Joseph Severn recorded his last utterances: "I shall soon be laid in the quiet grave—thank God for the quiet grave—O! I can feel the cold earth upon me—the daisies growing over me—O for this quiet—it will be my first."

It seems Severn had told Keats about the Protestant Cemetery and described its tranquil beauty. Now the two men lie side by side, their well-tended graves marked by simple stones. Severn outlived his friend by fifty years, leading a busy and varied life, including a stint as British consul in Rome. He was apparently not very good at this job, but his fine qualities as a human being were movingly celebrated by John Ruskin: "He understood everybody, native and foreign, civil and ecclesiastic, in what was nicest in them—and caught hearts of all in the golden net of his good will and good understanding." By a strange accident or oversight Keats's name only appears on Severn's gravestone. The poet's stone has an engraving of a lyre and carries the famous epitaph he wrote himself: "Here lies one whose name was writ in water."

Shelley's cremated remains, brought here after he drowned in a sailing accident off the Tuscan coast near Viareggio in July 1822, are buried in the newer, more crowded part of the cemetery, under a simple stone with the inscription "Cor cordium" (heart of hearts), and a story hangs on that. At some point between February 1821 and July 1822, the old section of the cemetery where Keats and Severn are buried, close to Caius Cestius's pyramid, was declared off-limits for future burials by the Pope. Next to Shelley is buried Edward John Trelawny, who supervised the cremation of Shelley's drowned body after it had been washed up on the beach, and the subsequent burial of his ashes in Rome. He thus performed a parallel role to that of

Severn, though Trelawny was a quite different kind of character, unreliable and self-aggrandizing.

Horace might have seen a reflection of his young self in the two young English Romantic poets, both Hellenists and idealists, mistrustful of Roman might. It's difficult to find references to Horace in their work. Shelley would certainly have studied Horace at Eton, though he clearly preferred Aeschylus and Plato.

As for Keats, you might think him an even less likely Horatian; but he seems to have studied Latin assiduously at Clarke's school in Enfield, even embarking on a prose translation of Virgil's *Aeneid*. To whom did he turn, consciously or unconsciously, when he sketched out one of the most celebrated openings in the whole of English poetry: "My heart aches, and a drowsy numbness pains / My sense as though of hemlock I had drunk . . ."?

Unmistakably the opening lines of "Ode to a Nightingale" echo the beginning of Horace's fourteenth epode: "You keep asking, Maecenas, why soft indolence makes me forgetful, in the deep heart's core, as though I'd drained some bowl bringing Lethean slumber." The imagery may be similar but the tone could hardly be more different, Horace urbane and self-deprecating where Keats is laceratingly close to the bone.

The Protestant Cemetery, which used to be in the middle of nowhere, now seems like a beautifully kept oasis in the noisy, lively, and chaotic southern fringes of Rome. On one side are artisan cottages and small studios, leading to the now fashionable quarter of Testaccio, where Rome's trendiest nightclubs burrow into a hill made entirely of broken amphorae. On the other, across a murderous road, is Piramide metro station.

Rome's unloved and unlovely metro suffers from extreme neglect and overcrowding; this is contemporary Italy's brutally ugly side, with no aesthetic uplift whatsoever. And to cap it all, a strange piece of propaganda is broadcast through loudspeakers; a "news item" about the *Playboy* founder Hugh Hefner, "still the playboy at 84." Perhaps he makes the contemporary Roman emperor Silvio Berlusconi feel young.

Somehow packing myself into the carriage, I clank through the bowels of Rome before being evacuated at Spagna. I have come to visit the one structure in Rome that you might think would capture the spirit of Horace better than the Pantheon, the closest there is to a stone embodiment of Horace's poetic and philosophic principles.

The altar of Augustan peace, or Ara Pacis Augustae, was finished just a year before Horace died, in 9 B.C. Having been moved a few hundred meters from its original position on the Campus Martius, a huge open space by the Tiber used ironically enough for military exercises, it now sits in one of the least-visited corners of the ancient city.

Dominating this site, but with surprisingly little presence, is the mausoleum of Augustus, a massive, low drum, built mainly of brick, overgrown with turf and wildflowers and ringed by cypresses and pines. A makeshift fence surrounds the enclosure; there are no grand statues or porticoes or announcements or plaques; the place, for all its size, has an air of neglect, and, strangely enough, of anonymity. It is as if no one quite knows what to do with it.

Of course Mussolini, fancying himself a latter-day Augustus, had an idea what to do with it. He instructed his architect Vittorio Ballio Morpurgo to create a pompous and lifeless square, the Piazza Augusto Imperatore, to link the Ara Pacis, for which Morpurgo created a new glass and stone building, to the mausoleum, in the process razing much of the neighborhood. No one seems to learn in Rome; this piazza repeated the mistake of the notorious monument to Vittorio Emanuele, an oversize monument to nothing, or to monumentality, and something Horace would have hated.

The Ara is now housed in a new purpose-built museum by the American architect Richard Meier. This building scarcely

deserves the scorn that has been heaped on it by certain architectural historians, and certainly not the mindless hatred of the
mayor of Rome who threatened to pull it down.

It is a structure suitably emphasizing lightness, grace, and
peace. Peace of course is at the heart of the purpose of the Ara
Pacis. Nothing about it is designed to overawe or intimidate; it is
the sculptural opposite of all Rome's famous triumphal columns
and arches. The main decoration consists of a double frieze, the
upper part portraying two solemn processions, one of lictors and
other officials, the other of members of Augustus's family, carved
not as noble ideals, as in the Parthenon frieze, but as recogniz-
able human beings.

At first glance the lower frieze looks like generalized flowery
decoration; and you might not even give it a second glance. But
the floral and vegetal friezes are works of great and subtle intri-
cacy; up to seventy different plant species can be identified here,
if you look with the attentive gaze of the botanist, rather than
the overhasty scan of the tired tourist.

Acanthus, mallow, asphodel, saffron, cardoon, bryony, grape-
vine, laurel, hedge bindweed, bellflower, fuller's teasel, arum, as-
paragus, date palm, anemone, ivy, iris, cornflower, honeysuckle,
carnation, wild garlic, water lily: all wind together in a symphonic
demonstration of nature's variety and abundance. They are the
sculptural equivalent of Horace's intricate, interwoven, lovingly
crafted odes (beautifully described by Nietzsche as "like a mosaic of words, in which every word, by sound, by position, and by
meaning, casts its influence to the right, and to the left, and over
the whole"), and like the Odes they are a celebration of natural
processes, of the regenerative powers and the ultimate unity and
beauty of nature.

The humanized version of the frieze is the great relief on the
east face of the altar showing a maternal figure with two babies
playing on her lap, flanked by two bare-breasted female attendants, one riding a swan and the other astride a sea monster.

Below them graze an ox and a sheep in a scene of natural abundance.

Am I convinced? Some of course would say the Ara Pacis was a monument not to peace but to military domination. They might recall the famous words from Tacitus's *Agricola*, put into the mouth of a heroic British resistance fighter: "They make a desolation and call it peace." Horace did his best to be convinced. What the Ara Pacis reminds me of most is the poetry of Horace's fourth book of odes, in particular the fifteenth and final ode, probably the last lyric poem Horace ever composed, addressed not to Maecenas but to Augustus.

At the heart of this poem is a vision of Augustan peace: "With you in charge of things / Augustus there will be no turn / to civil war, peace-annihilating violence / or the rage which makes whole cities quake." And then at the end comes a scene that could have been sculpted on the noble altar itself: "On ordinary days, and holidays, / we'll have street festivals, mothers / and their children too, well-stocked stalls / good food and wine to thank the gods for. / And we'll sing songs, remember those who died / defending us; the retreat from Troy / the saving of Anchises; the progeny of Love."

It is a moving and heartfelt conclusion to Horace's lyric oeuvre, and I don't doubt that Horace's praise and thanks to Augustus, whom he fought long before on the battlefield of Philippi, in the name of the old freedoms of the Roman Republic, are sincere. Horace undoubtedly feels the Pax Augusta is something worth celebrating, offering an immeasurably better chance of peace and prosperity to Romans, to Italians, to people within the bounds of an empire he no doubt saw as benign, than the preceding half century of violent civil war.

But I can't help feeling the poet has finally allowed himself to become too embedded, to will himself into the role and voice of the good citizen, rather than allow himself that crucial margin of error, that ability to be different, even dissenting, which he enjoyed when Maecenas, not Augustus, was his patron. And surely somewhere Horace must have had his doubts about an empire that depended on expansion and exploitation; and which extorted as its price, in the end, a lack of real freedom at home.

Ten

Religion, or How to Believe

I grew up in a dying religion. Or perhaps one that was already dead, though Nietzsche's report of the death of God had somehow failed to reach Farleigh House Preparatory School, where we were solemnly taught that God dictated the first five books of the Old Testament to Moses, that the wafer and the wine at communion became, not just metaphorically but literally, the body and blood of Jesus (the doctrine of transubstantiation) and that sex existed purely for the purpose of reproduction.

At Farleigh House, a rather eccentric institution where many of the boys were scions of the Catholic aristocracy, I accepted many strange ideas and rituals without question. On certain days we had mass before breakfast, an idea obviously unsuited to the metabolic needs of young boys. Two or three fainted every time, slumping to the ground with a thud. Not having enough to eat was a constant preoccupation. This, combined with a certain daring iconoclasm, led a friend of mine to break into the cupboard containing the large wafers used for Benediction, throw them on the floor (to desanctify them), and scoff the lot, washed down with so much communion wine (I think it was Cyprus sherry) that he became violently ill.

The discomforts and absurdities and occasional cruelties of this version of Catholicism were compensated by a sense of pride and specialness. We English Catholics were a superior breed— morally superior, apparently, though the evidence was all against this, and socially superior, in that we were a small sect within the already quite small sect of the upper-middle-class English.

For me this brought with it a complication: I was the son of a Catholic convert mother and an utterly unreligious, nominally Church of England father. The blood of true-blue Catholicism ran nowhere in my veins. Protestants, our teachers implied, were little better than heathens. But did that make my father, and my grandparents, inferior to my mother? It was a puzzle and a conundrum.

This strange mishmash of faith and snobbery, perhaps unsurprisingly, did not survive all that long after I arrived at Eton College, whose Catholic foundation in 1440 by the pious King Henry VI had long been overlaid by more worldly influences.

At Eton I experienced a crisis of faith. I could no longer believe chunks of the dogma I had been taught at Farleigh House. Some of them fell apart as a result of historical biblical scholarship. Painstaking research in different disciplines, including literary criticism, showed conclusively that the first five books of the Bible could not have been dictated by God to Moses, or indeed composed by the patriarch. The books dated from different periods.

Somehow this not terribly important-sounding piece of scholarship had far-reaching effects. It confirmed what I already suspected, that the pleasant tweed coat–wearing amateurs at Farleigh House had not really had a clue. We already realized that Mr. Callaghan, who was supposed to be teaching us science, but only succeeded in boiling alive some South African toads when he reset the thermostat in their tank, had few scientific credentials; but what if he had equally little idea of theology, on which the whole school was supposed to be based?

Behind it all was a vague but powerful idea of God; we were taught something about the Trinity but it was always God the Father, the character in a white beard, who held the key. There was reassurance in this figure, despite his punitive aspect; something to fall back on in times of intense loneliness. But God the Father began to drift away.

At the same time I could not embrace the thoroughgoing scientific materialism enthusiastically evangelized by my friend Gary Coulter; a cold world of atoms and molecules and dark interstellar spaces, entirely bereft of God, awaiting explanation by scientists.

Gary was a scientist in the making, and also a working-class boy from the north of England, the only one to be found at Eton at that time. Perhaps he felt lonely too—after all, he had even more reason to feel lonely than I did, he was farther from home in many senses—but found his salvation in cold, hard facts.

I was no scientist; I had little interest in or understanding of how anything practical worked: when asked in the science paper at my scholarship exam to construct a scientific diagram of a machine, I could only draw a childish picture. If I had read Wittgenstein at the time, I could have said "that the world is, not how it is, is the marvelous."

As it was I could draw little comfort either from the retreating symbols and beliefs of Catholicism or from the brave new world of scientific explanation, which did nothing to assuage loneliness. The only thing that could fill this heart-shaped gap was art—in particular literature and music.

They at least made me feel less alone. As I continued to learn the piano I began to grapple with pieces of real emotional depth and complexity, especially Chopin mazurkas and Schubert impromptus. I read voraciously. Devouring *War and Peace* at the age of fourteen, over two weeks of an Easter vacation at my parents' house, in my bedroom with its new green carpet, the smell of whose underlay has somehow always been synonymous with hope, was the most intense and mind-opening experience of my young life.

But there was still the official structure of religion at school, together with an aesthetic power and attraction. I couldn't help loving College Chapel, its soaring perpendicular vault; I was intrigued by the modern stained-glass windows by Evie Hone and Patrick Reyntiens (to designs by John Piper); and then there were the astonishingly vigorous, masterful fifteenth-century paintings rediscovered and restored above the choir stalls.

This particular version of religion might have seemed odd to Horace—religious observance was generally quite lax in his time—but the sense of growing up at a time of religious decline, skepticism, and confusion was familiar to him.

Official Roman religion, based on the Greek Olympian pantheon, was pretty much an empty shell, at least for sophisticated people, by the time Horace was born in 65 B.C. It had been hollowed out by centuries of skeptical intellectual inquiry, starting with the pre-Socratic philosophers and continuing through Socrates himself and the Socratic tradition, passing through Plato and Aristotle and branching out into the Epicurean, Stoic, Cynic, and Cyrenaic schools.

The chief intellectual, skeptical influence on Horace himself was clearly Epicurus (341–270 B.C.), founder of the Epicurean school, a thinker of extraordinary power and nobility grossly misrepresented in later ages as a proponent of lax hedonism. The Epicurean system had been magnificently rendered into Latin verse by Horace's predecessor Lucretius in *De rerum natura*, parts of which I studied as a schoolboy at Eton. Lucretius expounded the central tenets of Epicureanism, summed up in twelve Greek words that translate: "Nothing to fear in God. Nothing to feel in death. Good can be attained. Evil can be endured."

With a strikingly modern scientific objectivity, the Roman poet looked at such matters as what causes thunder and what position the woman should take in intercourse to ensure conception. Lucretius had much to say about love, some of it prophetic of later writers, especially Freud. Love, for Lucretius, is an immense and cruel delusion: love, even or especially in the heat of its fruition, is never stable or unmixed in enjoyment. There may be a kind of sadism at the heart of it. "There are secret stings which urge lovers to hurt that very thing, whatever it may be, from which those germs of frenzy grow." Love can never be satisfied: "So in love Venus mocks lovers with images, nor can bodies even in real presence satisfy lovers with looking, nor can they rub off something from tender limbs with hands wandering aimless all over the body."

Above all, Lucretius wanted to free his contemporaries, more superstitious than religious, of the unnecessary fear of death and of malevolent gods.

Though Lucretius comes across as a man of unremitting seriousness, there is a gentler and more humane side to the Epicurean philosophy he evangelized with such passion. Epicurus himself had been moved as much by compassion as by intellectual fervor. Epicureanism stresses the benefits of friendship and of the beauty of the natural world.

But very little of that gentle consolation comes through in Lucretius's version. What drives him is the intellectual or scientific passion and liberation of "knowing the causes of things," as Virgil would put it.

Horace's bent was different. Mere knowledge was never enough for him. Lucretius, his great predecessor poet, the magnificent expounder of the Epicurean system, had made one great mistake: in his fervor to save his contemporaries from superstitious fear of the gods, he had ended up creating another bleak dogmatic system.

The drive for knowledge can become a kind of obsession. Beyond that, it can reduce the world to ashes—to something known with the mind but not appreciated with the senses. The point was to live, to taste the day.

At a certain stage of his life, one can deduce, Horace was almost as ardent a follower of Epicurus as Lucretius. You might remember that Horace in his very early twenties was also an ardent follower of Brutus and Cassius. But by the time he comes into our view, as a poet in his thirties, Horace is too circumspect to be an ardent follower of anybody or anything.

One of Horace's most subtle odes portrays him as a reformed Epicurean. In a typically Horatian twist he describes himself as a former follower of "mad wisdom"—that is, not religion but dogmatic skepticism. Something has happened—thunder and lightning bursting forth from a clear sky—that disproves Epicurus's materialistic theories, derived from Democritus's atomism. According to Lucretius, thunder and lightning are caused by the action of clouds. So God, or Fortune, has power after all; or at least power to produce the unexpected, to shake the established order. Here's my very loose version:

SHOCK TO THE SYSTEM (ODES 1.34)

Not a regular worshipper of any god—
In fact something of a "militant atheist"
In my time—I'm having to backpedal

Because the crash has struck out of nowhere:
Thunder, which as we all know comes from clouds,
And the flash of lightning from a clear sky,

An almighty storm, shattering the peace
From east to west, with a shudder
In the planet's bowels, and tsunami

Sweeping everything away; nothing,
No one, nowhere is safe; the god Chance rules,
Maliciously; there's no security on earth.

The poem is not really about scientific theories of what causes thunder, but about the uncertainties and vicissitudes of human success, an implicit warning to the overproud or overmighty. No doubt that was why the Irish poet Seamus Heaney turned to this ode when considering the events of September 11, 2001. Heaney has come around to Horace late in life, but the man born on a farm in Derry, the countryman and republican turned Nobel laureate, has much more in common with the freedman's son from Venusia turned court poet to the emperor than do many more obvious Horatians.

The multiple levels and ironies of the not-at-all-simple ode have turned out to be peculiarly satisfying to the mature Heaney. Heaney has always struggled against being conscripted to any cause or sect, while his sympathies have remained clear. Born a northern Irish Catholic, he has not wanted to be narrowly defined by tribe, while not wanting to deny his origins.

The Horatian ode is a defense of the independence of the poet. In one of his strongest and most personal statements, at the beginning of the first book of epistles, Horace stakes out his independence like this: "You ask, who is my leader, my Führer, under what roof do I take shelter? I am my own man, not bound to any master's oath."

Odes 1.34 is subtle in so many ways. Maybe the most subtle part is the very first line, "Parcus deorum cultor et infrequens," "I a reluctant and infrequent worshipper of gods." What's subtle is partly syntactical: the reader doesn't quite know whether to take this line as a firm statement standing on its own or as going with the next line, "while I used to go around as an expert in a mad kind of wisdom."

As the wise and great Horatian scholar Eduard Fraenkel remarked, we need not deduce from this that Horace ever stopped being an Epicurean, of a kind. He was not a dogmatic Epicurean, like Lucretius, and he was not deeply interested in the scientific theories that fascinated his predecessor. He took what he wanted from Epicureanism, the parts that he found congenial: the humane emphasis on friendship and physical pleasures and delight in the natural world.

But then Horace also reserved the right to worship the gods even if only reluctantly or infrequently. Or at least he reserved the right to speak in deistic language, to use the names of the old Olympian gods not just as poetic flummery but with deep feeling.

Horace constructed his own personal Pantheon, nothing as grand and overarching and magnificent as Marcus Agrippa's splendid domed edifice in Rome. The big daddy god, Jupiter, does appear in Horace's odes, but there is nothing personal about him. He is more the force that cannot be gainsaid, the ultimate arbiter of things (so a bit like Augustus, I suppose).

Horace gets much more personal about certain lesser gods, and there is no doubt which god he feels about most strongly, most personally. Mercury, the winged messenger, the god of the lyre and language, the god of gain and commerce and trickery, is Horace's god. He says he was born under the sign of Mercury; because he is one of the "virum Mercurialium," the mercurial men, he has been saved from being crushed to death by a falling tree at his farm.

All Horace's feelings about Mercury, and about himself as a mercurial man, come together in one of the most beautiful of all the odes.

TO MERCURY (ODES 1.10)

Eloquent Mercury, Atlas's grandson,
You who gave voice to brutish cavemen,
Teacher of beautiful exercise,

You're the one I sing to, bearer of messages,
Supreme among luthiers, playful
Go-between of the gods, the joker.

You stole a whole herd of cattle, Apollo
Gave you an earful, then even he had to
Laugh, seeing you'd filched all his arrows.

You guided King Priam with his gifts to Achilles,
Helped him give the slip to all the Greek
Warriors, the destroyers of cities.

And you the conductor of spirits
Lead souls to their rest, gold-batoned maestro,
Ease our passage from higher to lower.

Mercury, or Horace's version of Mercury, turns out to be rather like Horace, in more ways than one. The apparently junior, unserious god, no match in power and status for the big boys, has some pretty impressive tricks up his sleeve.

Horace's Mercury is above all the god who gives speech, the eloquent one. No need to ask why the boy from Venusia rates speech and eloquence so highly. They were all he had—and hasn't he done well with them? Not only speech and eloquence are the gifts of Mercury, but music too, the music of the lyre, which also stands for lyric poetry. Here Mercury, the thief, seems to be standing in for Apollo; or rather he has stolen Apollo's thunder, he has stolen not just Apollo's quiverful of arrows but also his lyre.

Mercury, in fact, is nothing less than the god of culture—the force that gives beauty and polish, not just in the realm of the arts but in sports and physical training too, to the manners of men. In fact, you could say he is the force that makes men men and women women—the humanizing force. Without the arts of Mercury men are like wild beasts.

But this god of culture is anything but a grand, solemn, lofty figure. That figure sounds more like Apollo, so often portrayed in monumental sculptures, with his chiseled face and laurel crown and otherworldly expression. He would have been the personification of German Kultur, the force of sweetness and light, and utterly humorless.

Humorless is the last thing Mercury is. Mercury is an irrepressible trickster and joker, who even brings a laugh out of the solemn Apollo when he pulls off the amazing trick of stealing the sun god's cattle (it's a convoluted tale that involved making them appear to walk backward).

But then, just when you thought you had Mercury covered, the boyish trickster pulls off another transformation. Mercury has his solemn side, as a guide, even as a leader. He is the one who guides Priam on his embassy to Achilles, to plead for mercy, for the body of his son Hector, the climax and the most moving scene of the entire *Iliad* (which, by the way, has inspired a wonderful poem from another northern Irish poet, Heaney's friend Michael Longley).

Mercury is a guide in more than one sense. He keeps Priam safe as he walks unseen through the campfires of the Greeks, assembled before the walls of Troy, soon to destroy and engulf the city in flames. This can't help reminding us of that other, later ode in which Horace, greeting his old comrade Pompeius Varus, tells the story of how, thanks to Mercury, he escaped from the battlefield of Philippi. Mercury is Horace's protector, perhaps because he personifies the quicksilver movement of the poet's mind.

Horace, and Priam, have had to be quick-witted, skilled in the use of language. That means not just the deployment of cunning rhetoric but speaking from the heart. It is Priam's words, the inexpressibly sad words of a father who has lost all his fifty sons, and especially his son Hector, the great protector of Troy, killed in single combat with Achilles, in revenge for the death of Patroclus, that finally bring forth humanity from the implacable, ferocious Greek warrior.

Priam calls on Achilles to remember his own father, old, far away, unprotected, and Achilles breaks down in tears. As both men, the older and the younger, weep with different kinds of grief, Achilles commands that the body of Hector be dressed for burial, out of sight of his grieving father, so as not to distress him further, and returned to be interred in Troy.

This solemn moment, alluded to with Horace's usual glancing economy, prepares for the end of the poem, in which Mercury has become the leader of souls, the psychopomp, the one who conducts the well-deserving dead to their places in the Isles of the Blessed.

This last stanza has both an exquisite musical beauty and a deep mystery. It closes on something like a profound chord, linking the words for upper and lower, the glorious world of the gods on Mount Olympus and the dark Underworld of Pluto and Persephone: life and death. Mercury—and I guess that means poetry and Horace's poetry in particular—is a sort of magic conductor, easing the passage between higher and lower realms, between life and death. All this of course operates not at a literal level of doctrine or belief but at a metaphorical level, the level of poetry.

If you asked what Horace believed, I think you would get a slew of contradictory answers. He was not a regular or frequent worshipper of the gods; that sounds true and convincing to me. But he could write about, and write prayers to, particular gods with unmistakably deep feeling, not just Mercury but also Venus, the goddess of love; Bacchus, the god of wine; Apollo, the god of the lyre. Some things, certain kinds of feeling, of awe, of reverence, of wonder at the deep mystery of things, are best expressed in the language of the gods. Horace was in part a rationalist, an Epicurean, formed by the long tradition of intellectual inquiry stemming from Socrates and Plato. But he also believed in a divine something, *theion ti* in Greek, as Socrates and Plato themselves did, recalling Homer. At times he seems to believe in astrology, as when he writes in a deeply serious poem to Maecenas that their astral destinies are conjoined. At other times he pooh-poohs astrology, as in the famous poem addressed to the unknown girl Leuconoe that culminates in the command "carpe diem."

I don't think Horace believed in a literal underworld, with Charon the boatman, and Cerberus the hundred-headed guard dog, but he could poetically imagine them, and the throngs of shades listening spellbound as his predecessors and role models, the archaic Greek poets Sappho and Alcaeus, sang their undying songs of love and war.

Poetry, for him, was the way of ensuring some kind of immortality, the path to eternal life. Not the immortality of Quintus Horatius Flaccus, the short, plump, prematurely gray man headed for the grave as surely as all those others he keeps reminding of the inevitability of aging and death: Postumus, Dellius, the wife of the pauper Ibycus. No, not immortality for him, but something approaching immortality for the poems, more lasting than bronze, higher than the bulk of the pyramids.

So Horace can teach us how to believe: that is, humanly, inconsistently, not too dogmatically or fervently. In his most philosophical poem, he reminds us that the loftiest philosophy can be sabotaged by a bad cold. Fervor in religion is usually considered a good thing; what's the point of lukewarm belief? But Horace saw that fervent belief too often involved great sacrifices, too often sacrificed today for tomorrow, too often jumped over the present into some glorious millenarian future.

Sacrifices of animals, another part of Roman religion that may seem quite alien and cruel to us, feature quite often in Horace's poems. But they are only ever sacrifices of single animals, often described tenderly and with pathos, never more so than in the uncomfortably close-up description of the kid sacrificed at Bandusia. Horace makes clear what he thinks of hecatombs, of excessive slaughters of whole herds of animals, in the great poem addressed to Postumus; no amount of slaughter of animals will put paid to aging and death, or to wrinkles.

But overfervent religion tends to emphasize an even greater and more overarching sacrifice: the sacrifice of life to death. The religion that would be born in a distant Roman province just a few decades after Horace's death, Christianity, is a prime example.

Brought up in a peculiar version of this religion, I did not really begin to understand it until I started to study for the Newcastle Scholarship in Classics and Divinity in my last spring term at Eton.

Reading the Greek texts of St. Matthew's Gospel and the Acts of the Apostles with commentaries informed by historical biblical scholarship convinced me of something about my own religion I had not previously understood. The founders of my religion had believed in an imminent Second Coming. Socially marginalized, with little hope of substantive improvement in their lot, they had fervently believed that the world as it was would soon end and that a new, better, more just order would take its place. When Jesus at the Last Supper said, "I will not drink henceforth of this fruit of the vine, until that day when I drink it new in my Father's kingdom," he had not envisaged a long wait.

This explained so many otherwise puzzling things about the gospels—the lack of attention paid to so many aspects of the here and now, to the banalities of family life and working life.

Springing up in the generations after Horace's death, the new cult of Christianity filled a spiritual vacuum whose signs Horace could already discern. Despite Augustus's best efforts to restore traditional Roman religion and morality, the material and administrative success of the Roman Empire was accompanied by an increasingly chaotic spiritual emptiness. Christianity surged into that emptiness, offering its followers a shining vision of spiritual equality as a compensation for a tawdry, unjust materialism.

But that was in the future. In the meantime, for Horace as maybe for us, life remains to be lived, without any great renewal or spring tide of faith. Perhaps we too are waiting, as we have been it seems for a century or more, for the next "rough beast" to slouch "toward Bethlehem to be born." The tide of Christianity, which was about to flow in when Horace died, has now ebbed.

This does not mean there are not fervent flare-ups, of born-again versions of Christianity, and of the other Abrahamic faiths, especially Islam. Some surveyors of the contemporary scene see a militant Islam pitted against militant atheism. But somehow both the militant Islamists (unfortunately at times much more violently) and the militant atheists seem, to me at least, somewhat out of date. When the series of uprisings against authoritarian regimes that came to be known as the Arab Spring took place so dramatically in 2011, militant or fundamentalist Islam appeared to have little to do with them.

Militant or fervent atheists are concerned not just about the recrudescence of destructive forms of religion, but more generally about what they see as a new age of credulity, a tidal wave of new age beliefs, in alternative medicine, the healing power of crystals, undefined "energies," threatening to wash away the rational values of the Enlightenment.

But what if the greatest credulity of all is in the power of science? This is not to be antiscience, but to make the distinction pioneered by the great teacher and cultural critic Jacques Barzun between science and scientism. Barzun defines science as "the body of rules, instruments, theorems, observations with the aid of which man manipulates physical nature in order to grasp its workings." As such it has very little to do with the often contradictory set of popular myths and beliefs about the power of science to extend life indefinitely, bring about a utopia of peace and plenty, or lead mankind to destruction, which Barzun calls scientism.

To be skeptical not just about the claims of faiths but also about those of scientism is to court unpopularity from every side. This seems to me to be Horace's position, and one that, mutatis mutandis (in that lovely old Latin tag that means "with all the necessary changes owing to changed circumstances"), I am happy to share.

As usual, not so different from when I experienced my crisis of faith as a schoolboy, I find myself somewhere in the middle—not a paid-up member of any faith, but not a militant atheist or devotee of scientism either.

I dabble in Buddhism these days, attending courses in mindfulness and meditation, but I do so more in a spirit of pragmatism than of belief. In any case, Buddhism does not demand belief in any deity. Buddhists seem to have found better and subtler answers to the problem of the overactive, endlessly seething, self-deceiving mind than any of the West's religious or philosophical traditions.

I find that meditation works; mindfulness of the body and breathing give a grounding in which the endlessly restless and circling mind can quieten somewhat. It is subtle and delicate and very practical and nothing really to do with belief.

I think Horace might have approved; but in any case I regard him as an ally. Buddhism does not demand belief in an all-powerful deity, but Buddhists in practice worship minor deities, such as Guan Yin, the bodhisattva associated with compassion, whose statue sits on a sideboard in our dining room. Canny Horace is also a worshipper of small gods, as the Romans tended to be, whatever their attitude toward the big official deities.

Traipsing around the hard stone streets of Pompeii and Herculaneum, I found myself more touched by the lararia, the small household shrines, some decorated with mosaics and statues, than by the big official temples. I always liked the idea of the Lares and Penates, the old Roman gods of the household and pantry. They seemed to be the deep autochthonous deities of place—humble but also powerful, concerned not with grand ideals but with domestic necessities.

I think Horace liked the Lares and Penates too. He mentions the Penates a few times in the Odes, always in the context of homecoming or nostalgia for home. They exemplify the centripetal power of his poetry, always bringing us back home from the farthest outposts of empire.

I associate the worship of Lares and Penates with my own nature worship. I have been a sort of Green—I don't really like the term environmentalist, and I am not an ecologist, in the full scientific sense—since my very early childhood, when I became entranced by birds and by all the goings-on in the large garden of the house where I grew up. Quite early on I also became aware of the threats to this paradise; one of my earliest literary compositions was a piece about an oak tree in a field, home to all sorts of insects, birds, and animals, facing the axe.

Unfortunately I have seen the threats intensifying. My life has been accompanied by the funereal beat of environmental losses: the felling of forests, the pollution and overfishing of oceans; the ever-intensifying pressure on the natural world caused by the expanding and consuming human population: what some ecologists believe is the sixth great extinction of species in the earth's history, this time caused by human beings.

But I am not a fanatical Green. Certain strands of Green thinking disturb me with their icy fervor, their preference for wilderness over the *convivencia* of human beings with the natural world. I am chilled when I hear James Lovelock display little concern for the billions of human beings who, it seems, will have to perish to restore balance to Gaia. I remember Blake, who said "where human beings are not, nature is barren," and that other English Romantic John Keats, who discerned a deep connection between the human ability to love and the survival of the natural world. I hope I enact it in my own small way in our garden, where the loving if inept cultivation of shrubs and flowers brings insects and birds.

Once again I think of Horace as an ally of my small-scale greenness—Horace the devotee of place, the lover of his own countryside, the prophetic scourge of environmental destruction. No note in all the odes sounds to me more modern or more strange than the passage in the first of the Roman odes, one of Horace's grandest statements about his poetry's public role: "Even in the oceans the dumb fish feel it, they feel the world contracting, as concrete piers thrown into the deep divide the waters." There is something truly remarkable, unparalleled as far as I know, about this sudden shift to the point of view of the fish, this utterly arresting recognition that fish too are sentient creatures; they may even be more sentient than we are, more subtly aware of what happens when human greed and grandiosity go too far.

More and more I think that if a new religion emerges from the decay of Christianity and other world religions, it should be a kind of nature worship. None of the arguments put forward by climate scientists, biologists, and ecologists has halted or delayed the processes of environmental degradation; what we need, I am convinced, is an emotional reconnection with the beautiful world around us, far more beautiful, not to mention ultimately life giving, than all the synthetic substitutes we are so busy developing. The way to that reconnection, I am equally convinced, lies through poetry.

Eleven

Carpe Diem

"CARPE DIEM" (ODES 1.11)

Don't ask, Prudence, it's better not to know—
Correction, we can't know—what THE END will be.
You and I are doomed, yes, but the doom's an open one:
Don't trust the tipsters' tables, the wise-after-the-event
Predictors; we had better LIVE through it now—this
    winter,
If we're lucky, the next, some spring to come.
One day the sea will cease its raging at the rocks:
Not yet, I guess. Wisdom's what we need, and wine,
And the long, slow art of cutting back
For richer, later fruit. As we speak the seconds
Tick away; today is ripe for tasting;
Who knows what tomorrow's fruit will be?

Tu ne quaesieris—scire nefas—quem mihi, quem tibi
Finem di dederint, Leuconoë, nec Babylonios
Temptaris numeros. Ut melius, quicquid erit, pati!
Seu plures hiemes, seu tribuit Iuppiter ultimam,
Quae nunc oppositis debilitat pumicibus mare
Tyrrhenum. Sapias, vina liques, et spatio brevi

Spem longam reseces. Dum loquimur, fugerit invida
Aetas. Carpe diem, quam minimum credula postero.

Sometime around the turn of the millennium my relationship
with Horace took on a new urgency and intimacy. Kipling was
spot-on. I had come back to Horace twenty years after finishing
my classical education. I hadn't exactly forgotten Horace during
that period; he had been working on me at a subconscious level.

Now, suddenly, he surfaced. Looking through the notebook-
journals I've kept pretty religiously for the last two decades
(sometimes they seemed like the only thing holding me and my
life together), I see the irrefutable evidence: fragments and stanzas written in longhand, in Latin. The first I find is the opening
stanza of the first ode of Book 3, "odi profanum vulgus et arceo"
("I hate the vulgar crowd and keep aloof"), written down in a
café at Paris Charles de Gaulle airport just before taking an Air
France flight to Cuba. Next to it I had written down a fragment
of Proust.

That was the first of many trips, continuing into the present,
on which I carried with me the little red Loeb Library edition
of Horace's odes and epodes, as my vade mecum, talisman, and
touchstone. With terse Horace came expansive Proust; the tight
stanzas against the long, rolling paragraphs.

I went out to Cuba on a wing and a prayer, hoping to meet a
red-haired poetess who had told me she might, just might, be in
the lobby of the Hotel Sevilla in Havana at a certain hour, on a
certain date. Of course she wasn't. In a strange, abandoned but
heightened state, not sleeping, having more intense conversations than one might have in several years in England, I continued traveling around the elongated island that had somehow
detached itself from the normal course of history. I played
Schubert impromptus on huge white Russian pianos left stranded
in obscure museums and hotel lobbies. I found people who in

the perverse absence of material abundance and choice seemed intensely interested in fundamental human questions, in art and poetry.

Back in London, I started to work on translations of Horace. The poem I homed in on was "Carpe diem." Suddenly this familiar—overfamiliar?—little poem spoke to me with the utmost urgency and contemporaneity, as I suppose Horace intended that it should, throwing it into the future as what the Greek historian Thucydides called "a possession for all time." The way of possessing a poem, especially an ancient one, is to translate it, which means not just bringing it from one language into another, but, inevitably, as we live in our time and not another, bringing it from one time into another. In some mysterious way the words written two thousand years ago were coming alive, as if newly coined, and I was drawn to respond, and to give something back to the poem, by bringing it into the present.

I couldn't exactly say then why this poem spoke to me so urgently, why I had suddenly become receptive to it after decades of indifference. But now I think Horace was in some sense the counterbalance to the flame-haired poetess, to my caprice of flying out to Cuba on the off chance of meeting her, to my continuing hopes that she would come and live in my house, to the sequence of poems I had written about her called "The Rock and the Unguarded." He would have understood all of this; he had been through it all and come out the other side.

There were two ideas of poetry here, as I suppose there always are with relationships between two poets. For Jo, poetry was all molten, red-hot or white-hot lava, spewing up pure passion, her passion for justice, which swept over a landscape and reduced it to scorched earth. The scorched earth might eventually regenerate, become fertile again. The scorched earth was me.

I was the listener, the receptacle. But so much of it was

torture, anxiety. Horace turns it all around. For him poetry is like a dip in an ice-cold stream, clarifying, not enflaming. But his coolheaded poetry can be just as urgent as the molten kind.

There are no preliminaries here, no introduction. We are thrust into the middle of a conversation. Horace never more faithfully obeyed his own instruction, to begin "into the middle of things" (that's what "in medias res" literally means, with that thrust from the Latin "in" with accusative, "into," not the more static "in" with ablative, meaning the same as our "in").

The conversation may be one-sided in that we hear only the poet's words. But the whole poem depends on the unwritten question asked by the girl Leuconoe. It all arises out of her anxious inquiry, whose exact form we can only guess but whose gist is clear: how long have we got, you and I?

Horace's poem is a response, one of the most courageous ones we have, to anxiety and fear about what cannot be known, yet is known to be inevitable.

As always with his poetry it is a personal response, which doesn't mean confessional or autobiographical. The persons here may be fictitious ones, but they are persons all the same.

This is a second-person poem. "Carpe diem" begins in the original Latin in the most purely second-person way you could imagine, with the simple second-person pronoun "tu," "you" (singular).

"You singular" might sound like a well-worn grammatical formulation. For those of us who had grammatical rules drummed into us when we were young, it takes something to get back to the meaning behind the rule. You singular means you, just you and no one else, because you are uniquely and singularly you: this wasn't necessarily something they stressed at school, where we were not encouraged to read Martin Buber's *I and Thou*. But being a poem—and this is something only a poem or a fiction can do—Horace's "Carpe diem" is addressed both to a unique and singular you singular, a girl with the singular name, no doubt chosen because of its singularity, Leuconoe—and to all the other you singulars in the world.

I say only poetry or fiction can do this. I mean only poetry or fiction can create this sense of the singular you. Philosophy can't do it, because philosophy always wants to generalize.

This is a thoroughly personal poem, specific in that sense. You could say it is deeply grounded in personhood, that inalienable fact of being human. It is just as deeply grounded in the specifics of place, which we can no more get away from than the specifics of personhood.

The specifics of place are quite unusual here. We have come to expect Horace to be Cubist, not naturalistic. But here in this short, urgent poem there is not time or space for the multiple perspectives of the Soracte ode. Here we are in one place and one season.

The season is unequivocally winter; perhaps even the last winter of all: not unusual for Horace, but particularly stark here. And the place is by the sea, but I guess not an agreeable seaside resort, such as Baiae on the Bay of Naples, the most fashionable resort for Romans in Horace's day, and a place Horace himself liked to visit, but somewhere bleakly exposed to the full force and fury of the elements.

It feels remote, and deserted; and we happen to know that such places appealed to Horace. "You know what sort of a place Lebedus is," he writes to his friend Bullatius. "It's even more desolate than Gabii or Fidenae: but that's where I'd like to live, incommunicado, forgotten by my friends, looking out from land at the raging sea."

The setting for "Carpe diem" is given specificity by two words in the Latin, "Tyrrhenum," going with "mare," sea, meaning the Tuscan or Etrurian sea, and "pumicibus," related to the English word pumice, telling us about the particular geology of the rocks or pebbles the sea is bashing against. Pumice—hardened volcanic lava—is only found on the Italian coast in the vicinity of

Naples. Pumice is hard and spiky and perhaps that is why Horace comes up with this strange idea of the sea being weakened by all that crashing against the rocks or pebbles, when we know it's the other way around, and the rocks or pebbles are being eroded.

This is also a love poem, of a kind: somehow, and given the whole long tradition of Greek, particularly Hellenistic, poetry this comes out of, you don't imagine the poet and the girl with the beautiful, strange Greek name have come together, to this remote, wintry spot, just to have an academic discussion.

But again, to think of it just as a love poem, or a seduction poem, that the point of all this clever talk is just "to get the girl" is to miss the point.

The seventeenth-century English Metaphysical poet Andrew Marvell may be the closest thing to a truly Horatian English poet; his "An Horatian Ode upon Cromwell's Return from Ireland" is certainly the closest anyone has come to matching Horace's political poise. But Marvell's "To His Coy Mistress," surely influenced by "Carpe diem," is magnificently unlike Horace's original.

Marvell's poem ("Had we but world enough and time") is all about the young poet's randy impatience. It is a virtuoso display of lust, the desire to have, now, contrasted with the endless death of not having. The coy mistress, never named, is no more than an object of desire.

Leuconoe, though she never speaks, is a fully acknowledged human presence—fully acknowledged in the sense of her great, and entirely human, fear and anxiety which the poem sets out to assuage. The poem is full of her, full of the feeling of her, full of her feeling. Perhaps the poet wants to get her into bed, but he doesn't want to rush her there, in a spirit of impatience. Everything must proceed at the right pace, in the clear-eyed enjoyment of what life has to offer, here, now.

The impatience of Marvell's young lover, for all its splendidly inventive wit, has something fearful about it, or behind it: the sense of time's terrifying rush. Time, passing all too quickly, is there too in Horace's poem, referred to as "invida aetas." This personified version of time is envious—like the bald, bearded figure in Bronzino's *An Allegory with Venus and Cupid* in the National Gallery in London, enviously looking on while beautiful young people cavort in bed. This makes it much less terrifying and imposing than Marvell's "time's winged chariot," probably armed with scimitars sticking out from the wheels to cut down unwary soldiers, like the one belonging to Boudicca, that doughty British leader of resistance against the Romans.

If Marvell pushes Horace too far in one direction, by being too impatient, too grasping, then another later English poet, Matthew Arnold, in his most famous and beautiful lyric, "Dover Beach," pushes him too far in another direction, by being too gloomy, too despairing.

Here again we find ourselves with two lovers on or by a beach, with the rasping sound of the sea raking up or crashing against the rocks or pebbles, reflecting on hopes and fears for the future. Surely the parallels are too close to be coincidental (and Arnold for all his criticisms of Horace knew him intimately, and by heart).

But the ways the two poets write about their seas, or beaches, are instructively different. "Dover Beach" can't help evoking departure; Dover is the place you go to, usually, when you want to get away to the continent. Though in fact the poem was written on Arnold's brief and apparently happy honeymoon in June 1851, the couple in Arnold's poem seem on the point of flight (the last word of the penultimate line), elopement perhaps, but not content to be where they are. (Horace, on the other hand, has no plans to escape. Where would you escape to? Is escape, in the sense beloved of travel brochures, really possible?)

The lights of France may gleam invitingly, but it seems unlikely that life will taste any sweeter there for this couple. Life has lost its savor, betrayed its promises. "Dover Beach" turns into a poem about faith, or the loss of faith. And if anyone doubts the Horatian connection, remember that in his 1857 lecture "On the Modern Element in Literature" Arnold saw, unconsciously, his own lack of faith reflected in Horace: "If human life were complete without faith, without enthusiasm, without energy, Horace would be the perfect interpreter of human life."

The retreating tide (no tides to speak of on the Mediterranean!) comes to symbolize the ebbing tide of faith. This, for Arnold, is the orthodox Christian faith, the faith of his father, the famous muscular Christian headmaster, the faith that sustained him as a boy but that cannot sustain him any longer (though he continued all his life to profess an unorthodox Christianity).

The Christian faith, just about to burst on the unsuspecting Roman world as Horace wrote "Carpe diem," had ebbed for Arnold nearly two thousand years later, rather as the old Greek religion had emptied of meaning in the time of Horace.

How do you create a kind of faith out of the lack of faith? The question is the same for both poets. Arnold's answer—forgivably, you might say, for a man on his honeymoon—is romantic love. The poem ends with the two lovers clinging to each other against the huge indifference and confusion of the world—prototypes of so many other pairs of doomed romantic lovers in the century and a half to come, right into our own time.

But if, as the despairing poet-lover has just announced, the world "hath really neither joy, nor love, nor light," can that love be any more than another false promise? Matthew Arnold's friend Arthur Hugh Clough was more rigorous than Arnold when in "Dipsychus" he saw through the illusion:

"Oh Rosalie, my precious maid, / I think thou thinkest love is true / And on thy fragrant bosom laid / I almost could believe it too. / O in our nook, unknown, unseen, / We'll hold our fancy like a screen, / Us and the dreadful fact between."

The dreadful fact is that there is no God. But what if there is a multitude of gods, small gods of small things, all the small things of the world?

Horace may be "a sceptical man of the world," as Arnold rather disapprovingly put it, but he is also a man who loves the world, in all its fleeting, changing reality. Those who like Arnold want to believe in romantic love as the replacement for religion will be disappointed in him. For Horace, who never denies love's heady and dangerous pleasures, the greatest thing about love is the warm glow of companionable friendship, one of the saving warm glows the world offers. The key to them all lies in one small word, the word for day, *diem*.

The crucial difference between "Carpe diem" and "Dover Beach" is the difference between day and night. "Dover Beach" takes place at night, on a warm summer night, in the unearthly light of the moon, glamorous, propitious for romantic love, but also a time when fears are exaggerated, when nothing is seen in its reassuring reality; better for owls and ghouls than humans. "Carpe diem" is strictly diurnal, the poem of a winter day. The movement of the poems is opposite; in Arnold's case, from romance to despair, in Horace's from anxiety to clear-eyed enjoyment.

Most translations of "Carpe diem" have, as it were, seized on the verb: surely that is what is important, the decisive action of seizing, of making the most of it, of going for it. But what if the poem is really about the day, the diem, our diem: what if it is the little simpler word that holds the secret?

We tend to take days for granted; their space and span is not grand; if we receive a per diem it will not be a king's ransom. We look past them to tomorrow ("tomorrow and tomorrow and tomorrow"—a dreadful vision of days without meaning) or back, obsessively harping on the past, to all our yesterdays. But days are where we live; in that sense, days are our home. Days are human time; the time we can live with and in, the time of mornings, noons, afternoons, and evenings. Days are the moment that passes, but also the time given to us to live, and the time we give to others in sharing: an infinitely rich everyday gift.

Carpe refers to the way we live our day. This, in the original Latin, is one of those complex and subtle words with multiple meanings, both violent and gentle—though one thing the violent and gentle uses have in common is decisiveness. The verb *carpere* can be used of military columns advancing in battle, but here we are closer to the meaning of gather, harvest, or pluck, used of fruits, flowers, kisses.

Especially fruits, and especially the fruit of the vine. I can say that with confidence because just before Horace has issued his most famous exhortation, he has urged Leuconoe to "be wise, decant the wine, cut back long hope into small space."

The word for cutting back, *reseces*, is the word used for pruning vines. The talk of decanting the wine, the implied reference to pruning, have been discounted by generations of scholars as standard Epicurean hedonism, conventional stuff.

But we know for Horace wine was not a conventional prop, part of the usual scenery, but a profoundly life-giving and vital reality, and the central metaphor of his poetry. No wonder then that wine, or the harvesting of grapes to make wine, should be at the center of the phrase that sums up his philosophy.

Carpe is such a tactile, sensuous word. As you say it you can feel the form of the hand, gently curling, the sensitive fingers ready to pick, to pluck. Picking and plucking are not actions that can be undertaken with too much force or severity; they certainly cannot be rushed.

Picking an individual grape means encircling the globe of the fruit with your fingers, so gently that you do not burst it, but with enough decisiveness to remove the fruit from the stem.

It is a blissfully warm autumn day in Austria, on the great vineyard hill of Zöbinger Heiligenstein. I am up there with the vine grower and winemaker Willi Bründlmayer. Every now and then Willi stops and picks a grape. "Quite sweet but no real character." This grape sampling is no caprice: "You know my real job is grape tasting," he comments. "Wine tasting is just a hobby." Willi is waiting until the moment when the grapes are not just sweet tasting but express the unique, essential character of the terroir: when they are fully, truly ripe.

The whole process of wine making means immersing yourself in time. The winemaker cannot control or stand outside time, or the weather; cannot speed them up or slow them down. He or she must live attentively, carefully, in the time that is given. The time of harvesting is the most crucial of all the decisions the winemaker must take; and it is a matter of waiting for ripeness, for the fullest concentration of flavor in the grape. Wine is a profoundly natural product, a fruit of the earth, of a particular patch of earth; but it is also a human achievement. Using the mystery of fermentation, man turns the juice of the grape, a sweet liquid with no staying power, into a long-lasting vintage: a living product that, miraculously, matures at almost the same rate as human beings themselves, and in a comparable manner, gaining complexity and (as the Burgundians say) spirituality as it loses raw power and gross materiality. Wine is no more immortal than we are, but it can be born with us (like the jar vintaged in the year of Consul Manlius that Horace celebrates in Odes 3.21) and it can die with us. All this is a question, not of denying time, or trying to outrace it, like the young lovers Catullus and Donne and Marvell, but of immersing ourselves in it and dwelling in it.

When we immerse ourselves fully in time, which means in the rhythms of the day and the natural world; the feel of the seasons; the sound of the sea; and in relationship, in conversation, wine drinking, and lovemaking, time may be transformed from a horrifying rush into a pleasurable flow.

The horrifying rush, which is time seen from an inhuman perspective, becomes the enjoyable slow walking pace, the *andante con moto*, of human lived time. Or simply what Horace called the day, *diem*, which is always ripe for tasting.

All this for me connects with a phenomenon of our time: the philosophy of slowness, best known through the Slow Food movement but extending to other areas of life and living.

The Slow Food movement is a revolution based on the act of tasting, predicated on pleasure, not violence. Its founding act, like the publication of Horace's Odes, took place in Rome, and assumed the form of a protest, organized by the journalist Carlo Petrini, against the opening of a McDonald's hamburger joint at the foot of the Spanish Steps, next to the house where John Keats died. But Petrini did not drive a tractor into the fast-food outlet, as the French antiglobalization activist José Bové might have done; he gathered a group of Italian grannies who set up some trestle tables and loaded them with home-cooked penne.

Slow Food might seem frivolous, at least to Puritans. But it has gathered force in its twenty-odd years of existence and attracted over a hundred thousand members from all over the world, from Burkina Faso to Bangladesh. Its defense of the pleasure of food is also a resistance to the powerful homogenizing forces of agribusiness, a defense of local habits and usages, of varieties of tomatoes and potatoes and peppers and apples bred over centuries. It is a defense of the human, of the local and of nature, of cultural diversity and biodiversity, and I am sure Horace would have approved.

A broader Slow Movement has grown (quite slowly, it must be said) out of the fertile soil of Slow Food. This has happened especially in Horace's native land of Italy, where you can now find slow cities (Cittaslow), and, apparently, slow approaches to music and sex. Again you could look at all this as something essentially frivolous; but then it could also be surprisingly important, a necessary rallentando in the face of two centuries of accelerated growth and destruction of the environment.

What Horace is telling Leuconoe is this: everything that is needed lies at hand, if only we know how to taste and appreciate it. Spiritual sustenance comes from a winter view, the snow-whitened peak of a familiar mountain; from a beloved waterfall, with ilex growing from the rocks; from the apparent monotony of the sea's waves; from wine, the great heartener and restorer of spirits; from friendship and conversation; and from love, so long as we do not expect too much from it or grab hold of it with too much vehemence. Horace's way is the way of worshipping small things and small gods.

Twelve

Excess, or Enough

Horace's first book of epistles ends with an envoy—a sending-out of the book into the world, since repeated a thousand times ("Go, little book and wish to all / Flowers in the garden, meat in the hall" is how Robert Louis Stevenson begins his charming one). But this is the most outrageous and indecent envoy ever written. Horace imagines the book as a lecherous rent boy who can't wait to be sold, to be handled, to be used and abused. This is the frenzied stage of maximum availability on the open market. Eventually, Horace envisages, things will settle down a bit, become calmer and more decorous. The little book, in its long middle age, will be taught in schools, all over the empire, for centuries to come (as indeed it would be, together with Horace's other books, which was the main reason why Horace's poems survived the Dark Ages). And then, only then, when it has a wide audience in the warmth and calm of future time, will the book give a brief portrait of its author.

You will say, Horace tells his book, that "I was born the son of a freed slave, in modest circumstances, and stretched my wings wider than my nest; that I became friends with the leading people of the city, both in war and peace; that I was small in stature, prematurely gray, that I loved sunshine, that I was quick to anger, yet easily assuaged."

The sketch is minimal, deft, done in a few brushstrokes. It is,

in fact, even more like a photograph than a Chinese brush painting, because it carries a date; it is the portrait of the poet at the
age of forty-four. That is, it does not pretend to be an eternal,
timeless portrait, but one of how this man, this poet was at this
particular age. It is as modern as a portrait by Cartier-Bresson.

Because there are so few traits, each one is etched sharply
on the collective memory. They would not be unforgettable if they
were blurred, idealized, inaccurate. They are not noble traits, the
characteristics of a saint or hero or the improbable bard who
stands on the plinth in the Piazza Orazio in Venosa, or in the little
square in Licenza, looking toward the Sabine Farm. They are
particular, distinctive, unidealized, human. Of all these traits,
the one I share with Horace is the least noble of them all: "quick
to anger," in Latin "irasci celerem," which suggests our word irascible. Horace was irascible, he tells us, and so, unfortunately, am
I. It is not something I am proud of, far from it, and I don't imagine Horace was proud of it either. He softens the harshness of
this unadmirable trait somewhat by adding that he is equally
easily assuaged, *placabilis,* and I would say the same thing about
myself. I get angry too quickly but I don't stay angry for long.

This morning, just before writing these words, I have lost my
temper, had an irascible moment. I am trying to buy a plane
ticket for my partner, who, at the last minute, needs to fly out to
Ireland to witness that country's latest humiliation at the hands
of the IMF, or the European Central Bank, or whichever con-
federation of financiers wants its pound of flesh (to add to the
gorging on flesh they have already done). Nearly at the end of the
online purchasing procedure I find that the computerized system will not accept any of her cards because they carry a different name from her passport one. I swear and curse at the
implacable, inhuman system that will not hear any appeals. My
shouting disturbs her as she is speaking to a diplomat in Dublin.
I gather some loss of face may have occurred. She says I am impossible to live with. I say I am only trying to help. These stupid

electronic systems we regard as progress would try the patience of a saint. And so on.

What does being quick to anger really mean, I can't help wondering, having been born, unlike Horace, in the post-Freudian age of psychoanalysis and psychotherapy. Horace no doubt wondered too, and in another of his epistles he gives a terse definition of anger: "anger is temporary madness," "ira furor brevis est." Elsewhere he speaks of anger as a punishment one might bear, like being under the lash.

This is pure speculation, but I wonder whether the enormous expectations Horace's father clearly entertained of his brilliant son had some effect on that son's temper. Were there times when young Horace, under the strict protection of the self-made small businessman from Venusia who accompanied his boy to Rome, to make sure he avoided temptation, felt he was not doing enough to justify the sacrifices his father had made for him, trying to make sure he would not feel socially inferior (though of course he would always feel socially inferior) to the sons of equestrians?

Being hot-tempered is, I am sure, a quirk of nature as well as a product of nurture. My mother is hot-tempered as I am, my father and sister not at all. They are slow burners, not *irasci celeres* but perhaps not *placabiles* either.

But I think there is even more to be said about irascibility, Horace's and mine. In his poetry, the man famed for his equanimity, for his adherence to the "golden mean," or "aurea mediocritas" in Latin, is quite often angry. In fact the famous stress on equanimity is not the product of a complacent, smug superiority, as it came to be seen in later times, but of quite the opposite: a hot, violent temper constantly needing to be kept in check.

What angers Horace? Many things anger him: bores, who stick like burrs, who will not be brushed off; the appallingly numerous tribe of bad poets; the materialistic excesses of his age.

With the word "excess" we are getting closer to the heart of the matter. Horace is living in an age of excess in Rome. At least,

I suppose you could say, it is an age of peaceful excess, or what we might call overconsumption. The end of the civil wars, the defeat of the main foreign enemies, the establishment of a stable political order: all this has enabled wealth to flow in Rome. A good thing, surely? Horace is not so sure. Sometimes he sounds very grumpy about it; he fulminates.

A good place to start is the opening poem of his third and culminating book of odes. This third book marks a change of tone. There is not the self-sufficient delight in poetry itself you get in Book 1, whose first ode ends in the poet's modest, slightly comical apotheosis, as he bumps his head against the stars in the pantheon of poets. There is not the sense of balance you get in Book 2. At the beginning of Book 3 Horace gives us the weightiest, most serious poems he will ever write: the "Roman Odes," marked quite often by anger, outrage, disgust, and what Jonathan Swift, in the epitaph he wrote for himself, called "savage indignation" (*saeva indignatio*). He has become a "vates," the Roman word for the poet as seer, almost as prophet.

Sometimes in these Roman Odes Horace seems to lose his deft touch and become heavy-handed; not just heavy-handed but also hypocritical, as when the celebrant of light and easy love metamorphoses into the "disgusted of Tunbridge Wells" critic of lax morals. For me the low point comes when Horace attacks the young women of Rome for their skill at Greek dancing, inevitable prelude to a later career of adultery. And you could find all this not just awkward but also chilling, when you see how Horace's stern moral line fits with Augustus's moral reforms, culminating in the Lex Julia de adulteriis coercendis, which authorized the killing of a woman caught in adultery by her husband or father.

The first ode of Book 3 opens in uncompromising style: "I hate the common crowd and I keep aloof." Sickened by vulgarity, the poet wishes to re-create himself as "priest of the Muses," who will sing songs never heard before to young girls and boys, not yet corrupted by the moral decline he sees all around him.

What's wrong with the common crowd and their values? You get the sense of a sort of stifling by wealth. Obsession with status, the desire to have more, to build bigger: perhaps these are unavoidable results of an age of affluence. "Yes, it's true that one man plants his vines more amply across his estates than another, that one candidate for office can boast more ancient lineage or a bigger crowd of supporters. Yet deep Necessity allots the fates of high and low with impartial justice; Fate's great tombola keeps revolving every name." This last line has an inimitable vowel music in Latin—"omne capax movet urna nomen"—capturing the rolling, revolving motion of the urn that contains and turns around human destinies, as the word "omne," meaning every, is shaken up and returned almost to itself as "nomen," name.

No amount of wealth or luxury can insulate people from mental and physical pain, from guilt and an uneasy conscience, from decline and death. "When the sword of Damocles hangs over the guilty one, his feast of delicacies turns to dust; not the sweetest birdsong or sound of lutes will bring back sleep to him or her." Think Macbeth and Lady Macbeth; think Bashar al-Assad and his beautiful, pained-looking wife casting their votes in a sham referendum as his shells rip into the flesh of children in Homs; think Rupert and James Murdoch as their empire falls apart.

This somber ode looks still further into the future. Halfway through, as we have seen, Horace has a vision of the ocean itself contracting, of environmental destruction caused by an excess of wealth. He saw the blight of affluence two thousand years before scientists started to worry about the degradation of the oceans.

In the ode that follows the famous "Eheu fugaces" one, in Book 2, Horace, this time speaking not in the warm conversational tone he addresses to friends such as Postumus, but in a starker, darker style and key, laments the falling-away from the modest values and virtues that made Rome great. So far so boring, surely; just another exercise by a "praiser of bygone times" (one of Horace's immortal phrases).

Well, no actually. This is one of the many Horace poems that startles with its prescience. "Few acres now left for the plough, as the manors of the rich devour the land; everywhere fishponds bigger than the Lucrine Lake": Horace could have been describing, not the outskirts of Rome, or Naples, in 23 B.C., but contemporary China, or southern Taiwan, where I have seen precisely the scenario he describes: pretentious villas eating into the precious, life-giving rice fields of the Meinong river valley.

This is what happens when pure personal vaingloriousness is allowed to expand unchecked. No wonder Horace looks back to the time of Romulus, one of the founders of Rome, and stern old Cato, the embodiment of antique Roman virtue (and hater of all things Greek, which makes him an odd person for Philhellene Horace to be invoking), when "private wealth was modest, and the public good loomed large."

Is Horace just a propagandist here, a useful mouthpiece for Augustus's views about the undesirability of excessive private wealth, his desire for a return to Rome's founding values of hard work, sobriety, chastity, and thrift? Well, another way of putting that would be that Horace and Augustus actually shared a kind of moral agenda. Not without strain, for both of them. Augustus ended up banishing his own daughter Julia for adultery. Horace, the lifelong bachelor, surely didn't entirely go along with Augustus's legislation enforcing marriage. But there was a congruence at the heart of it—a shared feeling that unchecked private affluence was in some strange way impoverishing the whole society. Augustus's concerns with the lives of ordinary Romans and with beautifying the public realm were genuine, earnest, and practical: the famous boast that he inherited a Rome of brick and left one of marble was not without foundation.

The question of whether Augustus's quasi-imperial rule was a "Good Thing," in Sellar's and Yeatman's undying phrase, has gone on being debated through the centuries. No one put the two sides of the argument more sharply than Tacitus, writing at the beginning of the second century A.D. On the one hand, you could say that Augustus corrupted the free Roman Republic and turned it into a slave state. On the other, you could say that he had created a relatively orderly society, in which Roman citizens had the protection of the rule of law, provincials were treated with decency, and force was used sparingly. Horace, having fought for the doomed Republic, veered eventually toward the latter view.

One aspect of the excessiveness of his time Horace has great fun with is the religion of gastronomy. Two poems from the second book of satires treat this theme. Both are light, and neither of them is among Horace's greatest efforts, but they look forward into our time with uncanny accuracy. The second, and more amusing one, Satires 2.8, describes a dinner party held by a certain Nasidienus, a humorless food zealot. A succession of elaborate dishes is produced, including a pregnant lamprey surrounded by swimming shrimps: "This was caught before spawning," explains the host, in hushed reverence; "afterward the flesh deteriorates." The sauce to accompany this delicacy is mixed from the first pressing of Venafrian olives, garum (rancid fish paste) made from the guts of Spanish mackerel, and boiled five-year-old wine. Really, the current sultans of food elaboration, Ferran Adrià and Heston Blumenthal, could not do any better.

Then disaster strikes; the canopy spread above the table comes crashing down and covers everything in black dust. Nasidienus is not deterred and brings out even more recherché delicacies, crane legs and the liver of a white goose fattened on figs, but some of the guests have had enough and run off without tasting anything.

The point is about taking gastronomy too seriously, as a kind of religion or philosophy, and it is underlined by playful allusions to Lucretius's *De rerum natura*. Could Horace even be mocking Epicureanism? As with the theme of Horace and wine, it is not entirely easy to place the elusive poet. He praises simplicity, offers

Maecenas his own country plonk, but knows all about the better vintages, even has a few (many?) jars in his own collection.

Here is a question: was Horace really a vegetarian? Sometimes it sounds very much like it. The whole of Satires 1.6 has a personal intensity about it; this is one of Horace's most autobiographical poems, the one in which he expresses most clearly his love and admiration for his father, his gratitude to his friends Virgil and Varius, his feelings about his social inferiority to Maecenas. And in this great and revealing poem, there seems no reason to doubt Horace when he says that after sauntering "out to ask the price of vegetables and flour," he wends his way home to his "supper of leeks and peas and fritters."

That doesn't prove that Horace was always a vegetarian. In a much later poem, he alludes to a famous story of the meeting of two philosophers in Athens. The worldly, sybaritic Aristippus (founder of the Cyrenaic school and predecessor of Epicurus) came upon the misanthropic Diogenes (founder of the minimalist Cynic school) preparing his greens for supper: the great antisocial Cynic remarks, "If you had learned to put up with this, you would not be courting princes." Aristippus retorts, "And if you had learned how to get along with people, you would not be washing greens." Horace, in this epistle to Scaeva, is firmly on the side of Aristippus. Diogenes's stance of needing no one is an attention-seeking pose, as W. R. Johnson suggests, or a form of veiled aggression. "To Aristippus," Horace tells his friend, "every form of life was fitting, every condition and circumstance; he aimed at higher things but as a rule was content with what he had."

Horace was certainly not a doctrinaire vegetarian—he was not a doctrinaire anything. He also may have changed in the time between the early satire and the later epistle. But I persist in thinking that he was happy enough eating vegetables.

The hunger for more is never satisfied. This applies, as every good Buddhist knows, not just to food but to sex, to every kind of having. Not least, of course, to money. Let's talk about money, an obsession with which we assume to be a unique feature of our time.

Money was just as much at the heart of Horace's society, two thousand years ago in Rome. "O citizens, citizens, the first thing is to get money; morals after dosh." This is the rule, Horace tells us in his first epistle, one of the most truculent, surly poems he ever wrote, proclaimed from top to bottom of the arch of Janus— the portico of Rome's banking world (plus ça change). "It's the lesson sung by young and old alike. You have good sense, you know how to behave, you have eloquence and honor, but you're a few grand short of a million: you're a nobody." So what does Horace think of a society based purely on the values of money and status? Not much. "So who gives you the best advice—the one who says 'make money, if possible by fair means, if not, any way you can'; or the one who encourages and helps you to defy the slings and arrows of outrageous Fortune, to stand tall and free?" In this poem, addressed to Maecenas but in a very different tone from the exultant odes, Horace seems both repulsed and frightened by the materialistic values of the herd. "If the Roman people should ask me why I don't think and judge the way they do, even though I stroll the same streets and squares, why I don't follow them in their loves and hates, I'd make the same answer the cautious fox made to the sick lion: 'because those footprints frighten me; they all lead toward your den; none lead out of it.'"

What is the antidote to all this excess? Horace calls it "what is enough," "quod satis est" in Latin.

He meant this spiritually as well as materially; perhaps spiritually more than materially. The Latin word *satis* means something slightly different from "enough." From satis come our words satisfy and satisfaction. Enough sounds like a bare minimum, what you need to survive on, but "quod satis est" can mean "what is satisfactory," what is conducive to flourishing as well as to survival.

Asking what is enough is the opposite of always asking for more. Horace, in that prophetic first ode of Book 3, asks for nothing more than what he has, the Sabine Farm: a beautiful, comfortable place, of course, but not a palace. The poem ends like this: "Why would I exchange my lovely Sabine valley for more burdensome wealth?" This impulse against expansion, in an expansive age, has still wider implications. The Roman Empire grew (nearly doubled in size) under Augustus, but at the end of his reign (at least according to the historians Tacitus and Cassius Dio) Augustus counseled his successors to cease the endless, Alexandrine striving for more and not to expand the empire beyond its existing borders. Perhaps the succeeding emperor who understood this best was the cultured Philhellene Hadrian, who reversed his predecessor Trajan's policy of endless military conquest.

But Horace goes further than all that. In an amazing about-face Horace asks not that he should be given more but that he should be given less. One of the strangest passages in Horace comes in Odes 3.16: "The more someone denies himself, the more the gods will bless him with. In the nakedness of destitution, I make for the camp of those who have conquered desire, and, a refugee, prepare for my renunciation of the rich." To me this has a hint of desperation; beyond that, of self-loathing. Somehow the imagery, of a destitute, defeated man seeking the camp of the enemy, recalls Horace's experience on the field of Philippi; surely a moment when he came close to desperation. And I wonder what Maecenas must have made of Horace's desire to "leave the side of the rich," and his image of the miser as "a beggar amid great wealth."

In the culminating passage of his most philosophical book, at the end of Epistles 1.18, the poet has in a sense become that "destitute" person: he has laid aside his dazzling collection of masks, he has exchanged his beautiful, elaborate dancing Greek meters for the sober Latin hexameter, the meter of those serious old Roman poets, Ennius and Naevius and Lucretius. He is no longer inhabiting some quasi-Grecian fantasy world (like Claude Lorrain's luminous vision of classical antiquity) but living in his dear perpetual place, the Sabine Farm. And what he writes, in sober simplicity, is something like a prayer.

"Every time I refresh myself, body and soul, with a dip in my ice-cold local stream, the Digentia, which waters the high, frozen village of Mandela—what do you think I feel? What do you imagine I pray for, my friend? May I have what I now possess, or even less; and may I live, for myself, what life I have left, if indeed the gods decide to grant me any more; may I have a good supply of books and enough food for the year; may I be spared the torture of hanging on the hope of every uncertain hour."

Thirteen

In the South

I'm bypassing Rome on this Italian trip. I've started in Turin, for reasons unconnected with Horace, though ones I think he would have approved. I've been attending Terra Madre, the biennial Slow Food fair that brings together subsistence farmers from Ethiopia and Ecuador, Italian cheese-makers and Barolo makers, idealistic Americans who are growing vegetables on rooftops and setting up ecological primary schools in Chicago. It's a global festival not so much of gourmandizing, the kind of overelaborate gluttony Horace mocked, as of reconnection to the earth as provider. But at the heart of it is a celebration of Italian food and wine, which mattered a lot to Horace and matter to me.

My most memorable moment has been a wine tasting in which the octogenarian vintner Aldo Conterno, from Monforte d'Alba in Piemonte via a stint in California, has shown just two wines, two Barolos from his best vineyard, Cicala, in two vintages, 2001 and 2006. Conterno, who looks hardly older than when I visited him in Monforte in 1989, is an essentially modest man. "I don't exaggerate about techniques," he says. "Nature is by far the most important influence, the action of man a secondary factor."

More movingly, he talks about the role of luck. "I've been lucky in everything," he says, and proceeds to tell a story about his service in the Korean War. Heading to catch a plane for some leave, he and his comrades were delayed when their lorry broke down. They sat by the side of the road, cursing their luck, and duly missed the plane out of Seoul by a few minutes. They watched as the plane's engines failed and it crashed into a mountain, killing everybody on board. At this point the memory is too strong for the eighty-five-year-old and he bursts into tears.

Horace also knew about the role of luck, or Fortuna as the Romans called her, and repeatedly mentions his own lucky escapes, from snakes and bears on the slopes of Voltur as a child, from the armies of Antony and Octavian at Philippi, from the huge wolf that gave him a wide berth and the falling tree on his Sabine Farm.

Now I'm on a night train out of Turin, heading south, hoping my own luck will hold. I've booked myself on the slow train, in an ordinary compartment, for this eleven-hour journey. Nowadays it's possible to travel from Turin to Naples in less than six hours on a high-speed train, but I can imagine what that would be like. An essentially colorless experience, six hours of high-speed boredom, with no sense of being in any particular country or place, as much like being on a plane as being on a train.

This train at least feels like a train, and feels thoroughly Italian. It is used by Italians (I see no foreigners on board apart from myself), for journeys up and down the long peninsula that somewhere not quite defined, but around Rome, breaks in two, divides between north and south. I have been in the north and I am going south, and they are almost like two different countries.

Horace was a southerner; he never forgot or hid that fact, and I think that to understand him better I need to explore the southern half of the peninsula, which I do not know at all. I intend to visit the town where he was born.

One of my fears is that I will be robbed on the train, that it will be full of Neapolitan pickpockets and Calabrian bandits. This prejudice against southern Italy, against the whole Mezzogiorno as a backward land of mafiosi and peasants mired in poverty, is in fact quite recent. In Horace's time the south was not seen as poor or backward. In fact if anything the prejudice worked the other way around: the north was the land of the barbarians, while the south had long been colonized by the civilized Greeks.

In any case, there don't seem to be any Neapolitan pickpockets or Calabrian bandits on the train. As we are about to start our journey out of Porta Nova station just before nine o'clock, my compartment has only one other occupant, a man in his seventies. The man, quiet and dignified, is accompanied as he boards by a younger man, whom I assume to be his son. The son helps him load his case onto the luggage rack, they embrace briefly, and the young man leaves.

For a moment, as will happen repeatedly on this trip, the centuries, even the millennia, roll back. I see the younger man as Aeneas, his father as Anchises, whom Aeneas, the Trojan hero and founder of Rome, carried on his back from the flaming ruins of Troy. It's a momentary flashback; the man returns to the present, as a solidly reassuring presence.

Our relative peace and seclusion is too good to last. As the train lumbers down the western coast, from Alessandria to Genoa to Pisa, the compartment fills and then empties with an assortment of mainly young Italians. None is noisy or annoying. I sleep intermittently, sometimes able to rest my feet on the seat opposite, sometimes not. When daylight breaks, we are somewhere south of Rome, just the old man and me again. The train stops at an obscure station and people get off, quite casually, for the first *ristretto* of the morning.

Low clouds scurry across the sky; rain spatters the train windows. It's late October, and autumn has come to the Campagna. This is not the idealized vision of southern Italy I know from paintings by Claude and Turner, but something grayer and grittier. The first place I notice, jutting out into the Tyrrhenian Sea, is the bay town of Formia, which seems to have come down in the world since it was the smart Roman resort called Formiae—outside

whose gates, incidentally, the great Roman orator and intellectual Cicero was murdered. I can see signs of ancient grandeur,
a castle, a tower, but more evidence of what bedevils the Italian
south, jerry-built apartment blocks, unplanned ugliness.

Formia is a sign of what awaits me in Naples, where the train
arrives, more or less on time, an hour later. Turin and Naples are
roughly the same size, but in every other respect are wildly different. Turin has a planned orderliness, a sober symmetry of
squares, wide streets, and tramlines. Naples looks as if it has
been the target of a low-level terrorist bombing campaign for
decades.

You emerge from the incongruously modern, shiny railway
station onto the Piazza Garibaldi, which is not really a square but
a cross between a building site, a car park, and a souk. I immediately give up my idea of walking to the Hotel Caravaggio and hail
a cab. The first thing the cabdriver does is to switch off the meter. I protest mildly, whereupon the driver proposes a flat fee of
ten euros. Of course I have no idea whether this represents a good
deal, given the possibility of being stuck in a traffic jam in the
Piazza Garibaldi for half an hour, and I am tired from not much
sleep, so I give in.

From this point our relationship improves. I decide that my
taxi driver is doing his best in a broken, dysfunctional place. I tell
him, redundantly, that my Italian is not much good, but I speak
Spanish. "Neapolitans will understand you if you speak Spanish.
But anyway, here you need to speak Neapolitan." I think this
means more than just a language.

A little while later, when we are finally out of the seething
Piazza Garibaldi and into the narrow, dark streets of the *centro
storico*, he adds, "The only thing we have here is the weather."
But even the weather is not working today; we shake hands as he
drops me off in the rain in the tiny Piazza Riario Sforza and I
hand over the ten euros, feeling more sympathetic than aggrieved.

I have come to Naples primarily as a base for visiting Pompeii and Herculaneum and to see the treasures of the National Archaeological Museum, before I move on to Horace's hometown of Venosa. These are the best places, or so one is told, to get an idea of what the Roman world was actually like; to approximate Horace's time. But it had not occurred to me that being in Naples, in the contemporary, seething, chaotic city, might be the best way to get in touch with the Roman world.

Forget Pompeii, essentially a graveyard, a city artificially stopped, like a broken watch, an archaeological reconstruction, an elaborate ruse for tourists. But experience Naples, a fascinating living place, and a city that has been written and rewritten, as Parthenope, as Greek Neapolis, as the Norman and Angevin and Aragonese and Bourbon city, as the short-lived Parthenopean Republic after the French Revolution, as Roberto Saviano's grim Gomorra, the city in the grip of the Camorra.

I realize that I am living on a Roman street; my hotel faces onto the via dei Tribunali, which is the old *decumanus maximus* (secondary main street, oriented east-west) of the Roman city. Into this narrow Roman grid, where everything is both at right angles and at close quarters, as it was in Pompeii or any other Roman town, have been thrown the great bleached hulks of Christian churches, rearing up, quite out of proportion to their (Roman) surroundings. The biggest of them all, the Duomo, looms up behind the Hotel Caravaggio, blocking out half the light, requiring you to crane your neck to see its vertiginous buttresses.

I have arrived in Naples in the middle of a garbage crisis—a garbage crisis which some say has been going on for decades. People have been hurt in violent clashes in the town of Terzigno on the side of Vesuvius; from what I have gathered, locals are objecting to the siting of a huge dump within the Vesuvius National Park.

The effect is that Naples is suffering from an unsightly and unsanitary rash of uncollected garbage; black plastic bags of refuse are piling up outside the white marble facades of the Baroque churches. The city has lost control of its own excretions.

My first expedition, having dumped my luggage and brushed my teeth in the Hotel Caravaggio, takes me as far as the Gran Caffè Duomo. Here I choose a Neapolitan doughnut, incredibly rich and heavy, to accompany my cappuccino, which comes with the chocolate lovingly arranged into an elaborate pattern. I will come here every morning of my stay, charmed by the patron's refinement of manner, his beautifully old-fashioned courtesy, a sort of irony in the best sense, a kind of implicit shrug that acknowledges the imperfections of Naples, as well as by the excellence of the coffee and the *pasticceria*. Here, as in other Italian establishments, you exchange the Latin greeting *salve*.

This is the opposite of the American greeting, more like a command, "Have a nice day!" The Neapolitan *salve* acknowledges that your day will not be entirely nice, that it will be marred by many imperfections, from the lamentable absence of refuse collection to the annoying Vespas and delayed buses, to your own unavoidable, but perhaps controllable, swings of mood, but for all that will be a human day.

The Gran Caffè Duomo is almost the nearest I get to the Duomo itself; I do peer inside this immense marble barn but am put off by the vast and charmless interior, and not sufficiently intrigued by the strange cult of a statue that spouts blood.

A shortish walk up the via del Duomo and then along the via M. Longo leads me to the National Archaeological Museum, which houses one of the world's greatest collections of Roman antiquities, particularly finds from Pompeii and Herculaneum (though visitors beware: budget cuts mean galleries are frequently closed).

A reproduction of one work in particular has enticed me to this museum—the wonderful small painting of a girl or goddess scattering flowers, known as *Flora*, which serves as the cover illustration of James Michie's superbly accomplished translations of Horace's Odes published by Penguin Classics.

I have imagined a whole museum full of works as beautiful as this Flora, but in the event I find very little that matches her. The tiredness from a night with little sleep on the train is catching up with me as I stumble through immense galleries full of grandiose Roman statuary. It seems inflated, grandiloquent, and leaves me cold.

How well did some of these Romans know themselves? I find myself asking. Why did they need to give themselves this false Greek gloss (rather like the Victorians covering over their ruthless mercantilism with the pious fig leaf of the Gothic Revival)— false, that is, to the true spirit of Greece? The Greeks, however fractious and politically incompetent, were always utterly themselves, authentic in their art and architecture and their incessant arguing. The Romans were better at administration than at art and arguing. They were perhaps the first civilization to suffer from inauthenticity, from what Sartre called "mauvaise foi." Even Horace suffers from it at times, with his bad temper, his sense of being at odds with himself.

The objects and artworks that speak to me and move me are almost invariably small, delicate, domestic, realistic; frescoes of duck hanging from a string; two tied deer; a pine cone; the realistic portraits of Terentius Nero and his wife, and of a woman known as Sappho, who seems to have an inner life.

Best of all, though, is Flora or Primavera herself. She is a young woman in loosely flowing clothes seen from behind, on a green background, her hair braided, holding her basket in her right hand and gathering delicate white flowers in her left. That bald description does not capture what is most magical and graceful and affecting; the way she steps and moves, with her left foot planted and her right raised, while she turns her head to the left. Marvelously, I think when I revisit Florence a few months after this Naples trip, Botticelli managed to recapture this spirit and freshness and rhythm in the figure of Flora in the Primavera.

Life and movement; some kind of meeting of real and ideal: the qualities of the Roman Flora, and Botticelli's Flora, are also qualities of Horace's odes, with their dancing step, their magical, unrepeatable amalgam of Greek and Roman worlds. Fleetingly, while Maecenas, the greatest artistic patron of all time, guided the first Roman emperor, these worlds came together to create the finest and most delicate art the Romans ever produced, in poetry and painting and sculpture. It was a precarious balance that could not be maintained for long.

Most of the mythological scenes here—and how these Romans loved mythological scenes—are deadly dull; endless depictions of Dido and Aeneas, or the Rape of Europa. They are the equivalent of the innumerable lesser madonnas and martyrdoms that fill Italian provincial galleries and churches.

Suddenly I realize what genius it takes to reimagine and re-animate such stock imagery, as Horace managed to do in the Odes—by his own special method of radical reduction, of sharp sideways glimpsing—and as certain painters and sculptors of his time, now unknown and unremembered, also managed to do.

At the same time Roman art was evolving in quite a different direction. If there hadn't been the emphasis on Greek ideals and monumentality, the Romans might have developed an art like that of seventeenth-century Holland, a secular domestic art that celebrated the pleasures and objects and people and landscape of the human day. Horace anticipated that too, in his satires and his startlingly original epistles.

But really I can't take in any more. There is too much of all this. I have reached that point where new cultural experiences and stimuli, at least of the higher kind, cannot be digested.

Luck guides my steps. I chance upon the perfect place for lunch, a small, dark restaurant, La Cantina di Via Sapienza, haunted by professors and doctors, with delicious fresh bread, excellent thick red house wine, unbleached rigatoni in tomato sauce, satirical cartoons of Silvio Berlusconi on the walls. I would come here every day for lunch if I could. It's a deeply civilized, deeply Italian place, as civilized and Italian as Horace himself. I think I feel closer to Horace here in this unpretentious restaurant than in the Archaeological Museum, with its inflated statues and its bawling tour guides. A chatty bunch of young medical students with white coats and stethoscopes bustles in, to order their takeaway lunch. People are having real conversations here, or are simply being themselves. I notice a woman in her seventies, eating on her own, with a quarter liter of house white and a *piatto di giorno* of veal with roast potatoes; no holding back, carpe diem.

Next day I decide to go to Herculaneum, smaller, more intimate than Pompeii; somehow less daunting. Nothing could be less promising than Ercolano Scavi station on the Circumvesuviano railway. There are concrete walls covered in graffiti, jerry-built flats with forests of aerials. Oleanders have been planted in front of the concrete wall separating the tracks from the flats, but they are not flourishing. The whole area oozes neglect, even despair. I wonder whether it has ever recovered from the eruption of A.D. 79. Deep down, did people wonder whether it was worth building anything beautiful ever again?

The road down to the ruins is lined with undistinguished pizzerias and gift shops. Herculaneum itself, hemmed in by unplanned development on three sides and the Tyrrhenian Sea on the other, looks tiny, miniature, but there is something deceptive about its scale. The houses themselves are surprisingly large.

And what Herculaneum offers is glimpses: buckled mosaic floors, the delicacy of wall paintings, the amazing detail of stucco and mosaic work; the rituals of bathing as evoked by the well-preserved bathhouse. The sheer grace of things, of a place where everything had its grace; a glimpse of a high civilization, in many ways higher than the graceless neglect that prevails now.

Not just civilization but the whole life of the place came to an end brutally and abruptly here. The people gathered on the shore, hoping for rescue from the sea, or that the lava wouldn't reach that far, but their luck had run out. The hot gases from the volcano overcame them there on the beach. I think of that strange ode from the first book in which a drowned man asks a passing sailor to sprinkle three handfuls of dust on his corpse, and begins by recalling the fate of the great mathematician Archytas: "You too, Archytas, great measurer of the sea and the earth and the unnumbered grains of sand, you too have come to dust, under dust, by the Matine shore, and it has not helped that you probed the secrets of the universe with your dying mind."

In Pompeii, next day, my first impression is of how hard the stony Roman streets are. An hour's trudging and I need a pause, a cappuccino. In the café of the ruins I overhear snippets of conversation from fellow Britons, dutifully following the numbered sites in their guidebook: "We've done numbers 48, 51, 53; now here's 38, 39, 46" . . . "I can't remember what I saw an hour ago" . . . "But tomorrow's paid-for" . . . "We do so need Mary Beard."

I don't feel superior. I am also finding it quite hard not to make this into a rather dreary logistical exercise, ticking off the sites rather than entering into them imaginatively. And perhaps that is partly a matter of scale, something Horace understood so well. Pompeii is just too big to take in, at least in that military spirit. It's more like an epic, while Herculaneum has the intimate scale of an ode.

After the break, things improve for me. I find myself at the entrance to the brothel, with its famous erotic frescoes. A serious but puzzled-looking blonde English girl, ten or eleven years old, is asking questions. "So is it like a boarding school?"

"Not exactly," replies an older woman. "You'd better ask your mother."

A man I presume to be the girl's grandfather steps in. "It's a place of ill repute."

"That doesn't help," interjects the woman, tartly.

The poor man tries again. "For one reason or another, women were visited by men." I see the bemusement on the girl's face tighten into a frown, the frown of that age when one knows the grown-ups are being maddeningly opaque, the frown of *What Maisie Knew.*

The brothel occupies a rather small, cramped triangular building on the corner of two streets, a few minutes from the Forum. The five cubicles, with their masonry beds where the acts of love or lust took place, are functional rather than luxurious. Mary Beard, the clear-sighted, debunking classicist and author of the definitive book on Pompeii, hopes for the sake of the largely nameless women who worked here that the hard beds were "covered with cushions and covers." She notes that men were not ashamed to leave their names on the walls; over 150 graffiti still survive, some simply recording the completion of an act of pleasure, others also recording the name of the prostitute (Fortunata, Myrtale—with a Horatian echo, though the slave-owning poet would not have needed to patronize prostitutes).

On the whole Beard is not particularly impressed. "It is, frankly, a rather grim place," she writes. "It usually proves to offer the tourist only a brief pleasure. It has been calculated that the average visit lasts roughly three minutes."

The thing that strikes me about the brothel frescoes illustrating various sexual positions is how decorous they are—nothing sordid or hidden. The people pictured in the frescoes are portrayed as young gods and goddesses—or at least in frank enjoyment of one of life's pleasures. It seems to me better than much of what goes on in today's more diffuse and sometimes disembodied "sex industry." But then the testimony of no woman who worked on the streets of Pompeii survives.

I admire Beard but I want to take issue with her. Her book on Pompeii is brilliant on what must have been the physical reality of the place but I feel it leaves out something else.

You can't miss the physicality of Pompeii, the scores of bakers, little restaurants, bars, brothels (well, perhaps only one full-scale incontrovertible brothel, but many places where sex was on the menu), potters. But its spirituality, in the broadest sense, seems to me equally striking, the extraordinary emphasis on art, on painting, on decoration, on the need for the expression and communal experience of drama, for worship or acknowledgment of the numinous, not just in official temples but in the smaller household shrines, for remembrance of the dead, in handsome tombs with lettering still clear after two thousand years, for more complex initiation into mysteries. Beard wants to remind us all the time of the gritty reality, but Pompeii wasn't just gritty. It was beautiful too, and the love of beauty, in everyday as well as grand things, seems to me a great achievement and somehow connected with Horace, who wanted to bring poetry into the prosaic Roman world.

The next day, after a two-hour journey from Naples, I'm sitting outside Horace's house in Venosa, on a brilliantly sunny late October southern Italian afternoon. There is nothing very remarkable about this place; it's on a narrow street or alley in the sleepy old town. The only thing that might catch your eye is a beautifully carved piece of stone, perhaps a lintel, built into a later house; a piece of Roman stone. Otherwise the little street leading to one edge of the town on its steep but not very high ridge, falling down into a verdant, beautiful valley, is ordinary. A rusty bicycle leans against a low wall.

One other thing that marks this street and this house out is a framed extract from Horace, one of twenty or so that the town council of Venosa has put up in various places in the Città di Orazio (not a bad piece of municipal patronage, better at least than that practiced by the mayor of Aranjuez in Spain who decided to blast Rodrigo's *Concierto de Aranjuez* through the town hall's curdled speakers on the hour, every hour).

It is one of the most famous passages in Horace, the beginning of the fourth ode from the third book, the longest lyric poem he ever wrote. In this personal poetic manifesto Horace tells the story of how as a young boy wandering on the Mons Voltur, or Monte Vulture as it is called now, he fell asleep on the mountainside and was kept safe from bears and snakes by a screen of leaves woven by doves.

Of course it's an unlikely tale, and Horace signals as much, I suppose, by calling the doves "fabulosae" (fabled); he's spinning a yarn as they wove the leaves; but it's not just blarney either, it's like a beautiful legend that has a grain of truth. I'm sure Horace did wander as a boy on the slopes of Voltur, the only big mountain around here, looming up twenty kilometers or so to the west, not out of range for an energetic youngster. And I am sure there were bears around then, and there are still snakes.

And maybe he did fall asleep one day on the wooded slopes of Voltur (I will go there myself, and find the "trackless" mountain disappointingly covered in telephone masts) and woke in a panic, and then realized he was safe. This feeling of safety, an unlikely safety, a safety won against the odds, is one of most profound feelings and gifts Horace has to offer. I'm feeling it myself now as I perch on the stone step, waiting for the custodian. In a small way I've made it too; survived not bears or snakes but Neapolitan drivers and tunnels through the mountains. I've reached a place I could call the beginning, or the end, of the pilgrimage safe and sound—or reached a place where I can just be, quite contentedly, in the here and now.

For Horace the story of his mountain adventure and preservation is a chance to rededicate himself to poetry, or the Muses who represent poetry. Because poetry is what in a larger sense has saved him and kept him safe. I feel it has kept me safe also; I make a little vow to rededicate myself to poetry, or at least to give it its full value in my life.

The volunteer custodian from the Venosa Archaeological Society, a pleasant and efficient woman in her forties, arrives with the key to the house. The bolt is rusty and has not been drawn back for quite a while, so I lend a hand or a bit of masculine brute force. Inside is a circular space, rather cool and dark, with the floor below the present street level. You can see that the lower layers of masonry, up to five or six feet high, are Roman, in the diamond-patterned opus reticulatum and the horizontal opus latericium.

This is the bathhouse of a private residence. Of course this isn't Horace's house at all. Even the enthusiastic custodian has the honesty to describe it as the "so-called" Casa di Orazio. But she explains that it is in the right quarter of Venosa, because Horace describes the view going out over two valleys. And she adds something about Horace's father's house, after he sold it, having been bought by someone who constructed a private bathhouse. So it could be Horace's house after all.

The interior has been re-created as a triclinium, or formal dining room, using a technique the custodian calls "archeologia sperimentale." I am not sure this is a technique, at least in any scientific sense, more a form of wishful thinking. There are various reproductions of Roman items, a couch, musical instruments, amphorae, and a portrait, draped in red satin, of the poet sitting and writing at an elaborate stone desk.

The portrait is pure kitsch, but I also find it touching (if not as satisfying as the pizza oraziana, topped with chunky local sausage, I will eat the next day in the pizzeria in the main square). Dressed in a white tunic with an embroidered blue cloak clasped over his right shoulder, his balding head crowned with a laurel wreath, Horace holds his stylus in his right hand, while he presses down on a scroll of parchment with his left. Behind him, presumably painted on a wall, two half-naked figures stand on plinths; one is a slender girl, the other a boyish figure with a shield over his head who looks like the god Mercury. Horace looks up and away, into the middle distance; his face is weathered but not battered, middle-aged (of course); an enigmatic smile plays around his firmly closed lips while his dark brown eyes have just the hint of a shine, of sadness mixed with wise and open acceptance, of the rare tear shed for Ligurinus.

Later, that evening, I am sitting down to dinner at the restaurant Baliaggio on the ground floor of the Albergo Orazio. I have come not just to eat (though the food turns out to be magnificent) but to give thanks. I have landed on my feet here, in every way you could imagine. Horace's hometown might have been a dump for all I knew; I had never heard of anyone visiting it. But Venosa is charming, laid-back, slow; everything I could have wished for. The Albergo Orazio, housed in a handsome palazzo, with fine eighteenth-century murals in the breakfast room, is a real find. It turns out to be run by a Horace enthusiast. *"Orazio è sempre attuale,"* she tells me as I leave. Horace is always relevant. My simple room has a lovely view, over weathered tiles toward a honey-stone belfry straight ahead, and then to the right, down a steep slope planted with olives, a sudden transition to rusticity, with herds of goats in the valley bottom and kestrels and jackdaws swirling above. Horace's hometown has a Horatian feel.

I order a half bottle of wine—not just any wine, the local wine, Aglianico del Vulture, grown on the volcanic soil around Horace's childhood mountain and vinified on the outskirts of Venosa. I choose the cuvée called Carpe Diem (what else?), from the 2005 vintage. It has an enticing rich nose of tar and leather, just a whiff of something wild and untamed; sweet lifted fruit on the palate. And to go with it, as a starter, a mixed antipasto locale, hot olives, ricotta with honey and walnuts, a plate of sausage and ham, mozzarella on a bed of lettuce, grilled aubergine and courgettes, strong sheep's cheeses, *melanzane parmigianino*, delicious and not overdone. My main course is *tagliata di manzo ai porcini*, quite a fatty but wonderfully flavorful cut of beef with a sauce of porcini mushrooms, sliced fine. I am going with Aristippus and Carlo Petrini, not Diogenes and Jonathan Safran Foer, tonight. "My God you can eat well here," reads the last sentence of the day in my journal. Perhaps I have finally learned something, something Horace teaches, something I should have learned years, decades ago: to take what comes with a "grateful hand."

Fourteen

Alas, the Years

I have to admit that I'm relieved to be here, at journey's end (almost), or at one journey's end, in the bland surroundings of Naples airport, almost the only place in Naples that could be described as bland, where, you might think, nothing could happen. The tension of traveling, that constant heightened state of awareness—which comes from being on the move, in unfamiliar and possibly unsafe places, where it is more likely than usual that you will lose possessions, or even yourself, or important parts of yourself, particularly if you are as absentminded as I am—has finally unwound. That means that I am not thinking about lax security procedures at Naples airport, or any of the myriad crazy people in the world who might be planning to blow up my plane.

Here once again, for the first time in days, because I feel relaxed, having dropped off my hired car unscathed, and even filled it up at a gas station underneath the Naples ring road, and somehow got back onto the ring road; having checked in my luggage, passed through security, I manage to sit down and enjoy an ode.

Odes and airports seem to go together. I can see why airports call for odes—something to fill their emptiness, the aching spiritual void of waiting. This void is nowadays filled mainly by shopping malls, a development that Horace would have deplored, though it would not have surprised him in the least. But

why an ode should need an airport, now that is more of a
mystery.

I am sitting and waiting and I open the book of odes, or
rather it falls open, somewhere in the middle. In the middle of
the middle, on the page that holds the fourteenth ode of the second book, opening with one of the most famous lines in Horace,
in Latin, or in any language, "Eheu fugaces, Postume, Postume."

EHEU FUGACES (ODES 2.14)

Oh the years, the years, just slide, dear Postumus,
My friend, and no pious observance
Puts paid to wrinkles, or the advance
Of age, or to indomitable Death.

However many hundred bulls you slaughter
You won't appease implacable Lord Pluto,
Who confines the strongest kings and those
Who in their day were giants, inside the moat

We all, dear Postumus, must cross, that's all
Who've fed on fruits of earth no matter
If we ruled as masters of the universe
Or labored in the fields as humble serfs.

We can congratulate ourselves on our
Escape from civil war and accident
From the damp south wind in autumn
Which brings infection to the lungs;

One day we'll have to face the black and sluggish
Styx and those condemned to endless
Pain, the rolling stone of Sisyphus,
Danaus' cruel daughters, those murderers.

The earth, our home, our dear, our loving wife
Are only lent to us and must be left behind
And all those trees you've planted far and wide
Will outlive you, all except the cypresses;

And your prized wines, all those grands crus
You've cellared, under lock and key,
Your oh so worthy heir will glug the lot
And stain the floor with your exquisite vintages.

You can sum up the message of this poem quite simply, and indeed the Loeb translator C. E. Bennett, in this 1914 edition, does so with his subtitle (not provided by Horace) "Death is inevitable." The interesting thing, the fascinating thing, is the distance between this statement, which is a classic instance of the truism, a statement so obviously true as to induce nothing but a yawn, and the truth, the deep poetic truth, of Horace's poem. This deep poetic truth is already present in that deservedly famous first line. "Eheu" means "alas," the dictionary will tell us. Anyone who has ever heard a Greek tragedy performed in Greek will know the Greek word *oimoi*, reserved for those moments when the unspeakable has happened.

"Eheu," like "oimoi," is more a sigh than a word (you have to say it out loud, ey-hey-oo, to get the full force of this), a visceral expression of regret, drawn up from the depths of a person's being or bowels, from the bowels of the earth where we all go.

Eheu fugaces. Alas how quickly, how fleetingly, how so fast that we can't really grasp them the years slide by . . . And then the master stroke, that repeated Postume. Postume is someone's name, a friend of Horace's, we presume, in that vocative case, used for calling or addressing, which we may know from the most famous vocative in Latin, Julius Caesar's "Et tu, Brute." But the repeated Postume is the opposite of the single, accusing

Brute; it is a complicit, rueful, companionable, arm-around-the-shoulder vocative, not a backstabbed one.

Postumus is very important to the poem even if we don't know much about him, as apparently we don't. He could be all sorts of different Postumuses, which is in a way the point. His name is an uncomfortable kind of joke; Postumus means "last," or "last-born," or posthumous in the sense of being born after a father's death. We tend to use posthumous for works published after a writer's or composer's death. This particular ode will not only outlive Postumus, and Horace, but us too, and generations of readers into the future.

The repeated "Postume" is more than a joke. It establishes address and context, the crucial fact that this is not some disembodied piece of moralizing but a fragment of embodied, dramatic conversation, addressed to a friend (the word "amice" comes later). We are always already embodied, in time and in relationship; so the phenomenologists and existentialists taught us, but Horace knew it long before Heidegger and Merleau-Ponty. Horace's particular relationship with his friend Postumus sets the tone for the whole poem. It is affectionate but not uncritical, and we can deduce that Postumus was one of those wealthy Romans Horace likes to take to task, in a friendly sort of way. Only a wealthy man could hope to appease death by the kind of extravagant sacrifices Horace describes.

It seems Postumus prides himself on his piety, pietas, God-fearingness you could call it, or orthodox religious observance. Horace does not exactly mock this, but he just states the facts; no amount of religion puts paid to wrinkles, to ever-advancing old age, to death, which no one has conquered.

Religion and wrinkles. It's a brilliant juxtaposition. Wrinkles are the one thing religion can't deal with. They are below it, in a way, beneath its notice. Religion in its high seriousness disdains wrinkles, the way our flesh folds on us, how the once wonderfully tight membrane becomes loose and baggy.

Maybe because of his unflinching awareness of wrinkles, sacrifice enough, the burnt or baggy offering of our youth and beauty, Horace had an aversion to unnecessary and excessive sacrifices. None could be more excessive than the ones he envisages Postumus making, hecatombs, or super-hecatombs, slaughtering three hundred bulls a day.

None of this will do any good, apart from the harm it will do to the bulls. In one of his most delicately lovely odes, I'm remembering, Horace tells the country girl Phidyle there is no need for sacrifices at all; crown the small images of the household gods with sprigs of rosemary and myrtle, the herbs that grow on the hill, and all will be well.

In an even more beautiful poem, the one addressed to the spring of Bandusia, placed at the beginning of this book, Horace brings us uncomfortably close to a sacrificial victim, a young goat whose horns are just budding, all ready for love and war, but all in vain. Those horns will never harden, those ruttings and rampagings will never happen. He really makes us feel what is involved in a sacrifice. The sacrificial victim is partly Horace himself, the man who sacrificed himself to the fierce taskmistress of poetry, sacrificed some of his happiness, the nice wife he might have had and the children to carry on the family name his father raised up from the low ground of slavery.

Horace and Postumus may have differences, different kinds of piety, different religious observances, different degrees of wealth and social class, but they are friends and fellow humans.

I've got to this point in the ode, and I have one of those embarrassing, tearful moments. People (if they notice or have any interest) will think I've suffered a bereavement, or broken up with my partner, when in fact I've just been moved by a perfect line of poetry.

Horace's way of saying he and Postumus are fellow humans is of heart-stopping simplicity: "quicumque terrae munere vescimur." He and Postumus form part of a we, the "we, all of us, who feed on earth's gift," or "gain our nourishment from earth's bounty"—which is far too flowery a translation, but then putting it too starkly doesn't quite work in English.

There is nothing high-flown about this in the Latin. The word *vescimur* means nothing more, or less, than "we eat," "we feed." Human beings are not defined here by any higher function—cogitation, philosophical thought, singing and playing the lyre, praying to the gods—but by that prime necessity of all created beings. We are eaters, earthy eaters. Even consumers, if you like, which I don't, actually, because it doesn't suggest anything as real or nourishing as feeding, but some more abstract compulsion that can never be satisfied.

Eating unites all humans, of all degrees and classes; the we is further defined as "kings and humble peasant farmers." We are equal as we eat, just as we are equal in the face of death, a point Horace drums home incessantly in these poems. If you wonder why, remember that they are addressed to the wealthy class at Rome by a man who came from a humble background, a fact he never hides and indeed wears as a badge of pride. Equality mattered more to him than to any other Roman poet.

Eating brings us down to earth, close to earth, earth we sprang from. There is nothing in the end we love more than earth. Horace is a great earth lover.

But that makes the end of the poem even more gut-wrenching. All the earthiness, the groundedness we love, which here he calls "tellus," not "terra," a word that can mean the whole orb, the globe, the green planet, as well as the soil we stand on, all that—including our home, "domus," and our loving and pleasing wife, "placens uxor," whom Horace did not have but I guess Postumus did, and the best bottles of wine in our cellar (which Horace certainly did have)—must be left behind, relinquished by us.

I'm noticing once again how wine figures in Horace's poetry, how it is no accident that this affecting poem ends with a stanza about wine. Wine is the richest symbol of what he has called earth's gift, the distillation of what the French call terroir into a liquid with quasi-miraculous properties and powers.

This Caecuban wine in Postumus's cellar is Rome's premier grand cru, the equivalent of Château Lafite, say, very select and very expensive. This is a rich taste Horace can entirely understand, because he is one of the greatest wine lovers of all time.

The Caecuban wine, better than the stuff they serve at pontiffs' banquets (I wonder what they serve at the Vatican these days), kept so carefully under lock and key (under a hundred keys, Horace says, with a touch of hyperbole), will end up staining the floor at some drunken orgy conducted by Postumus's "worthier" heir. Bachelor Horace seems particularly ill-disposed toward heirs. He will end up leaving his estate to the princeps, which means to the Roman people. This is the other sacrifice in the poem, bitterly humorous, the bloodlike deep red wine poured over the floor, less violent than the hecatombs at the beginning but no less wasteful and pointless.

So what is it, I am wondering now that I have reached the end, that makes this poem so much more, so much more moving, than Bennett's bald summary? Quite simply, the three-word summary tells us what the poem is about while the poem itself, with its inimitable music, makes us feel the truth of what it is about.

We/I know perfectly well that "death is inevitable," but we/I would rather not think about it, let alone feel the truth of it. That was obviously just as true in Horace's time as in ours, even if the means of keeping it at bay were sometimes (not always) different. A philosopher might invite you to think about the inevitability of death, but Horace is a poet, not a philosopher (or he is a poet-philosopher). The poet invites us to feeling.

As so often in Horace, a conversation between friends is the context for the thoughts and feelings that matter. Unlike his predecessor, the Epicurean philosophical poet Lucretius, Horace is not setting out a philosophical system and explaining "the nature of things" and what our attitude to these things should be— death should be nothing to us, because we will not feel it when it comes. That may be true but it is not precisely the point. How does it feel, knowing we are mortal?

The poem begins with the sharing of feelings about the passing of time. The quick, fugitive gliding by of the years is something we only notice when we get to a certain age. Everyone knows that time suddenly speeds up when you get to forty or so; a year to a child, the distance to one's next birthday, is an immense, unimaginable expanse of time, and rightly so, because the child will be a different person next year, maybe six inches taller, two shoe sizes bigger.

But to a middle-aged person a year is no time at all; nowadays I find myself constantly caught out by the way a year has passed since my last meeting with someone, seemingly in no time at all. A year to a fifty-year-old is like a day to a five-year-old. This immensely dramatic, almost all-important fact of life is something scientists and philosophers have had remarkably little to say about. The scientists have little to say about it because it is not objectively verifiable. Scientists will tell us that time, objectively speaking, passes uniformly, except perhaps when you are traveling at the speed of light, but we aren't very often.

The nineteenth-century French philosopher Paul Janet, to give him his due, did attempt a mathematical explanation of our subjective sense of time's speeding up, with his logarithmic theory of proportionality: as a proportion of the time we have lived, five years for a fifty-year-old are equivalent to one year for a ten-year-old. But that doesn't quite do it, because then days and minutes would also speed up proportionately, and they don't. As Horace knew. It's the years that slide by, not the days, not if we live in them and taste them.

Time of course has been passing as I have been reading this ode, and the day is heading toward evening. All this time I have been in the departure lounge, that strangely named place that might be all too apt a symbol of our existence, the dramatic and final notion of departure incongruously paired with the dated, bathetic lounge, suggesting a tranquilized relaxation. Time may speed up and glide by us, but here time almost stands still. For once we have more of it than we would really like. We, my fellow travelers and I, that young Spanish couple, the grandmother trying to control an unruly two-year-old, the English family with their three children, are held in transit, in a kind of nonplace, certainly not a home.

There is nothing much to distract you in the departure lounge; maybe you can eat a sandwich and drink a beer, as I have just done, but such distractions quickly pall. Left alone with the bare facts of your existence, with nothing to take your mind off your imminent departure, with that anxiety which Heidegger believed revealed Being to us, you might just be more authentic than you are in your well-padded and insulated existence. And Horace's deceptive ode, for all its sympathy and beauty, is no more ultimately reassuring than Heidegger's existentialism. Like Heidegger, it takes everything away from us, the familiar props, the earth (I am about to leave it, trusting myself once again to rivets and engineers and pilots and air-traffic controllers), our home, the person closest to us—leaves us with that black stream, the wandering river of Hades, we must all one day cross, and then what?

I am back home, late at night, in the comfort of my own house, which always seems a little strange after being away, in my own bed, with my partner, lying awake, perhaps overstimulated by everything I have seen over the last couple of weeks in Italy.

In the London dark, which is never completely dark, I am reassured by the regular, peaceful sound of Ching Ling's breathing, like some underground river that flows and will flow. But not forever. The terrible thought comes that one day that breathing, and mine, probably on another day, earlier or later, will cease. Nothing can make that thought unterrible, but Horace's ode at least bears witness to one who had the courage to think and feel it, two thousand years before I did, to say it and sing it as a friend, in the lucid and lovely words that go on shining with their modest glow, like a warm candle in the darkness.

A view of what may have been Horace's villa, outside Licenza

Acknowledgments

This book arose out of friendly conversations, begun at Trinity College Cambridge when we were students and still continuing, with George Myerson. We had originally conceived of a cowritten book, but that proved difficult to pull off. Most generously, George suggested I take the reins on my own; so the book assumed its present quasi-autobiographical form. But it is thoroughly infused with his brilliant ideas and perceptions.

The title of the book stresses my relationship with Horace, but that relationship has been mediated by the work of countless others—of scholars, who have preserved and edited the texts of the poems, of poets and other writers, whose relationships with Horace have inspired and illuminated my own efforts. Among recent writers on Horace, David West, W. R. Johnson, Peter Levi, and David Armstrong have been especially useful.

I also owe a great debt to Jonathan Galassi at Farrar, Straus and Giroux for believing in the project and overseeing it sensitively and wisely. I am extremely grateful to my agent in the United States, Peter Bernstein, and his wife, Amy, for their unstinting support, advice, hospitality, and friendship. Miranda Popkey has guided the manuscript into print with tact and good judgment.

Thanks go to my friends Richard Addis and James Burnett-Stuart, who read parts of the manuscript and offered comments;

to my family; and above all to Ching Ling, who has lived with it, and with me, and assisted with encouragement and incisive comments the slow process of turning an idea into a book.

A final note: my father, the wine merchant Philip Eyres, died on December 6, 2012, a couple of weeks after I had finished my final revisions. He had read some chapters in manuscript; I am sad that he could not live to see the book in print.